A Family Remembers
GERMAN–JEWISH LIFE FROM
1848 TO 1926

A Family Remembers

GERMAN–JEWISH LIFE FROM
1848 TO 1926

Translated and with an
introduction and epilogue
by Michael Brodnitz

Copyright © 2017 by Michael Brodnitz
All rights reserved.

No part of this book may be reproduced or used in any form or by any means, electronic or mechanical, including photocopying, recording, scanning, or by any information storage and retrieval device or system, without prior written permission from the publisher.

Published in the United States by Long Sky Media, sending out signals from the island city of Alameda, California

ISBN: 978-1-946588-00-5

Find us online. LongSkyMedia.com
Send us a note: editor@longskymedia.com

Printed in the United States of America

CONTENTS

Introduction vii

Chapter 1: Julie Badt Herzfeld. 1
Chapter 2: Julius Brodnitz 75
Chapter 3: Hedwig Herzfeld Brodnitz 123

Epilogue: Julius and Hedwig Brodnitz 197

Appendix A: Julius Brodnitz's Speech,
    Delivered in August 1930. 213
Appendix B: Notes Dictated by
    Julius Brodnitz, 1934 217

ACKNOWLEDGMENTS

THIS PROJECT TURNED OUT to be more complicated than I expected. From deciphering the cramped, nearly century-old Gothic German handwriting to translating narratives that assumed a great deal of nearly lost knowledge, I turned frequently to others for help.

I would like to thank Dr. Jürgen Matthäus of the United States Holocaust Memorial Museum in Washington, DC, who was so kind as to transcribe Julius and Hedwig's handwritten narratives, making it possible for me to translate their observations.

I would also like to thank my friend Werner Schlieper who helped me understand some archaic German terminology and the nineteenth-century German education system.

I would like to thank my wife, Gaya, for putting up with me while I hid for many long hours in my "office" while working on these translations. Gaya was of great help in reading copies of my rough drafts and offering many suggestions that improved the translation. Special thanks also to our son Dan who helped by guiding my rough draft into a readable version and kept encouraging me when I was ready to abandon this project. Without their help, this translation would never have been completed.

Thanks also to our daughter-in-law Barbara for organizing the publishing process, and to Elisabeth Beller and Jessica Bernstein for their valuable editorial work, Helen Bruno for her book and cover designs, and Tony Jonick for his layout work, all helping to bring these slices of life to you from almost another world, to convey the similarities in outlook, drive, and independence across generations.

INTRODUCTION

THIS VOLUME BRINGS TOGETHER three personal narratives, short memoirs written by Julie Badt Herzfeld, Julius Brodnitz, and Hedwig Herzfeld Brodnitz (daughter of Julie and wife of Julius). These collected memories provide a glimpse into the life of a German-Jewish family as the nineteenth century transitioned to the twentieth and approached World War II. These works were translated from German and annotated by Michael Brodnitz, great-grandson of Julie and grandson of Julius and Hedwig Brodnitz. Michael has also written this introduction to their stories.

The Memories of Julie Badt Herzfeld (1907)

Imagine a world without television, radios, telephones, or the Internet. Or think of a time when airplanes, high-speed railroads, or even cars did not exist. When electricity had recently been harnessed but humans had not yet figured out what to do with this new invention. Coal was king, and heat and energy for both homes and industry were generated by burning it. Europe of those days was dominated by a few big empires, which were ruled by kings, kaisers, czars, or other hereditary heads of state. And most of the world was owned as colonies by a handful of European powers. This is the world into which Julie Badt was born in 1848 and in which she lived most of her life, until her death in 1914.

Julie's family lived in the eastern part of one of those super powers. Imperial Germany was formed when the many small principalities of Central Europe were absorbed into the German Confederation. This powerful kingdom was led by Prussia and included major portions of what was the Kingdom of Poland. Poland had the misfortune of being situated in territory surrounded by three of the Continental powerhouses: Germany, Russia, and the Austro-Hungarian Empire. These three powers conspired to absorb Poland, which they proceeded to do in three steps during the years 1772 to 1795.

Generally the Jews who had lived in the portion of Poland that had been absorbed by Germany had adapted rapidly to their new country and its language. Under prevailing German laws most of the Jews were allowed to live only in segregated sections of the major German cities. These sections were known as ghettoes. Residing in other towns required special permits. These permits were usually granted only to one or two families in each location. Nonetheless, as Julie tells, these isolated families maintained their special customs and culture and followed the traditions of the Jewish religion.

One consequence of the isolation of the Jewish families in the smaller towns in eastern Germany was that the scattered families put extra effort into keeping in touch with their dispersed family members. Consequently, cousins and other relatives often married other members of the family. This is clearly noticeable in Julie's story when she talks about how she married Abraham Herzfeld while her brother Louis got married to Abraham's sister Nettchen Herzfeld. We also know that in the next generation, three of Julie's daughters (Rosa, Hedwig, and Bianka) married three Brodnitz brothers (Hugo, Julius, and Hermann).

During Julie's life, the rate of infant mortality was still extremely high. Four of her ten children died in their pre-teen years. Of the six remaining offspring, two died without leaving heirs. The remaining four children gave Julie and Abraham eleven grandchildren and a multitude of great and great-great grandchildren.

In spite of this dramatic growth in the number of Julie and Abraham's progeny, it appears that, as far as we know, none of Julie's children or grandchildren perished in the Holocaust. This is rather amazing, considering the fate of other branches of the family and the lot of European Jewry. But that is a different story altogether.

Introduction IX

This translation of Julie Badt Herzfeld's *Memories* is dedicated to her grandchildren, who were very young when these *Memories* were written. They cherished Grandma Julie's story enough to bring a copy of it with them to their new homes, wherever fate carried them.

The Memories of Julius Brodnitz (1926) and Hedwig Herzfeld Brodnitz (1923, with a 1931 Addition)

During my childhood in Tel Aviv, two pictures were always on display in my parent's apartment. One was a large drawing of a distinguished-looking, bearded elderly gentleman. The other was a photograph of a dignified gray-haired lady. My mother told me that these were pictures of my father's parents, neither of whom was alive by that time.

Mother told me that Grandpa Julius was one of the leaders of the Jewish community in Germany until his premature death in 1936. I also learned that shortly after her husband's death, Grandma Hedwig moved to Palestine, where she rented a small apartment near my parent's apartment in Tel Aviv. Unfortunately, Grandma Hedwig died in 1938 while visiting her two older sons in New York City. As I was only three years old when Grandma Hedwig died, I have no real memories of either of my Brodnitz grandparents.

In the fall of 1947, my father sailed on his first business trip to the United States. During the Jewish New Year holidays, in September 1947, Mother took me to Jerusalem for a weeklong vacation. While in Jerusalem, we joined a tour of the Hebrew University campus on Mount Scopus. The guide took us to look at several laboratories and ended the tour by showing us the university's library. There he demonstrated how researchers used the library's new card catalog system to locate items from the collection. By pure chance (at least I believe that it was unintentional), he picked from the catalog a card that led him to the library's copy of a newspaper called the *C.V.-Zietung*. This weekly newspaper was published in Berlin during the years before World War II by an organization for which Grandpa Julius had served as President. The specific issue that was retrieved was the issue from the week of Grandpa Julius's death. In the center of the front page was a picture, framed in black, of Grandpa Julius. It was a copy of a big picture that was hanging on the wall of my parents' living room. That was when I first realized that Grandpa Julius had been an important leader of the Jewish community in Germany. I also felt for the first time that I had missed much by not having known my grandparents when I was at an age at which I could have benefited from their lives and experience.

There was something unique about the generation of Jews who were born and raised in small towns in the eastern provinces of Germany during the second half of the nineteenth century. Most of these people were born into families that they described as "rich in children." Families with eight or more children were not uncommon in that generation. They considered themselves to be both German and Jewish. Many of their families belonged to the upper middle class at a time when Germany was newly unified and was becoming a world power. Because the authorities in Germany had recently lifted many of the restrictions on the country's Jewish residents, and because of their parents' growing affluence, many of the male members of that generation were among the first of their family to attend either a university or a higher technical school. This opened new career opportunities for my grandparents' generation in fields such as medicine, economics, and engineering. (Higher education for young Jewish women did not become widely accepted until the next generation.)

Following the death of my parents, we were faced with difficult decisions as to how to dispose of the contents of their Tel Aviv apartment. Most was given away to relatives in Israel or to charities. We decided that the accumulated letters and pictures were to come with us to the United States, pending further review.

Both my wife and I were still working at that time. We therefore shipped the documents to New Jersey and set them aside for later review. Several years passed before we finally started to organize this collection of letters, pictures, and books into manageable files. Among the first items that caught our attention in this accumulated memorabilia were two volumes of typed personal narratives, entitled *Memories*, written by Grandpa Julius and Grandma Hedwig Brodnitz, my father's parents.

Grandpa Julius dictated his *Memories* in June 1926 while he was sitting for a portrait by Professor Eric Wolfsfeld. The painting was commissioned by an organization with the long German name *"Centralverien deutscher Staatsbuerger juedischen Glaubens,"* better known by its abbreviated name *"der C. V."* This name roughly translates to the "Central Union of German Citizens of the Jewish Faith." The C.V. was, at that time, one of the largest Jewish organizations in Germany, with a paid membership of more than 60,000, or approximately 10 percent of all the Jews living at that time in the German Republic. The mission of the C.V. was to challenge in the courts of law all anti-Semitic or discriminatory acts. Grandpa Brodnitz had joined the C.V. shortly after he moved to Berlin and opened his law office around the year 1900. In 1920, he was elected president of the C.V., a position that he occupied until his untimely death in 1936. Julius' portrait was commissioned by the C.V. to commemorate his sixtieth birthday (August 19, 1926).

Julius wrote that he had dictated his *Memories* without having at his disposal any underlying documents. Nonetheless, his story is rich with facts and observations that shed light not just on the history of the Brodnitz family, but also on German-Jewish culture of that era, starting in the early years of the nineteenth century with tales about his own grandfather Leib Brodnitz. Leib was born in 1792 in a small town called Schwersenz, near Pozen. The district around Pozen had been part of the Kingdom of Poland. It was annexed by Imperial Prussia during one of the three "partitions" of Poland by Prussia, Russia, and Austria during the eighteenth century when Poland's three larger neighboring countries divided that country's territory.

When Grandma Hedwig initially wrote her own *Memories,* she said that they were intended only for her husband. This version was apparently written at about the time that Julius was dictating his own story. In 1932, with the help of her new daughter-in-law, Susi (my mother), Hedwig expanded her story and prepared additional copies of it for her three sons. She also added to her *Memories* a listing of her siblings, with their birth and marriage dates.

Regrettably, the stories of both *Memories* ended several years before January 1933. After that date, on which Hitler and the Nazi Party gained control of Germany, the lives of the Jews in Germany were never the same again. Consequently, neither story tells about the dramatic events that followed that date. This is especially regrettable, as Grandpa Julius continued to play a leading role in the life of the German-Jewish community during the early years of the Nazi era until his death in 1936. We did come across several letters and other documents that helped shed some light on Julius' role in the events of that period of time. Other documents and diaries reached us when we closed the New York City apartment of Fritz and Henny Brodnitz. Fritz, the oldest son of Hedwig and Julius, was the last of the immediate family to leave Europe, in 1937. When he left Germany, he took with him some key documents as well as Grandpa Julius' diaries for the years 1933 to 1936. The translations of some of these documents can be found in the epilogue and appendix B.

Once I started working on the translation of my grandparents' *Memories,* I realized that the task was more difficult than I had originally imagined that it would be. For one, the language Grandpa Julius used was rather sophisticated and, in some places, a bit dated. For example, in describing his school days, Julius used grade designations that have long gone out of common use in Germany.

Another difficulty resulted from the traditional German tendency to write long and, at times, rather complicated sentences and paragraphs. I took the liberty of breaking up some of these segments into more readable English without, however, changing the content of the original text.

Julius dictated his *Memories* without having any supporting documents, and his tale assumed that the reader would be familiar with the family names and dates that he mentioned in his narrative. I would like, therefore, to add some of the missing data for new readers.

Julius' Grandparents and Siblings

The oldest member of the Brodnitz family about whom we currently have detailed information was Leib Brodnitz, Julius' paternal grandfather. Leib was born in 1792 in the town of Schwersenz. Leib married Caroline Holz, who was born around the year 1800. Caroline died in 1886 and Leib died in 1893. Both died in the city of Posen.

Eight of Leib and Caroline's children lived to adult age:
1. Roeschen (dates of birth and death unknown)
2. Dorothea, 1819–1901
3. Samuel, 1823–1896
4. Nehemias, 1824–1902★
5. Michael, 1826–1895★
6. Max, 1828–1905★
7. Isidor, 1839–1899★

8. Benak (Barnett), 1841–1873**

* Buried at Weissensee Jewish Cemetery, Berlin, Germany

** Buried in Queensland, Australia

Julius's father, Samuel, was born in Schwersenz, near Posen. His mother, Rosalie Weissbein, was born in the town of Bromberg, Germany, in March 1831. Rosalie died in Posen in September 1894. Both Samuel and Rosalie were buried in Posen.

Samuel and Rosalie had twelve children, nine of whom survived to maturity. Samuel wrote in ink in his father Leib's old Hebrew prayer book (dated 1837) whenever a child was born. These notes list the names of each child in both German and Hebrew and the dates of their births, in accordance with both the Gregorian and Hebrew calendars. When a child died, the child's name was crossed off in the prayer book and the date of the death was added there.

The following children of Samuel and Rosalie survived to adult age:

1. Hugo, 1854–1914
2. Felix (Nehemia), 1856–1880
3. Alfons (Aharon), 1857–1929
4. Fanny (Rachel), 1860–1912*
5. Julius (Yakov), 1866–1936**
6. Martin (Michael), 1867–1923*
7. Selma (Leaha Rachel), 1870–1930
8. Margarethe (Ester), 1872–1940*
9. Hermann (Chaim), 1875–1958

*Buried at Weissensee Cemetery, Berlin

**Buried at the Jewish Cemetery in Potsdam, near Berlin

Hedwig's Grandparents and Siblings

We have limited information about Hedwig's family. From the memories of her mother, Julie, we know that Hedwig's paternal grandparents were Moses Herzfeld (1807–1887) and Bluemchen Levy Herzfeld, who died in 1882.

Moses and Bluemchen had several children. Abraham Herzfeld (1838–1907) was Hedwig's father. Abraham's sister, Jeanette (Nettchen) Herzfeld, married Julie's brother, Louis Badt.

For a list of Julie's children, see page 74. For a list that Julie's daughter Hedwig created of her surviving siblings, see page 195.

The years after Julius and Hedwig wrote their *Memories* proved to be most challenging to the Jewish Community in Germany and Europe as well as for the whole Western World. The Stock Market Crash of 1929 followed the German hyperinflation in the 1920s. Three years later, in January of 1933, Hitler and the Nazi Party rose to power in Germany. During this whole period, the comfortable middle class existence of Julius and Hedwig slowly disintegrated. Their son Otto Brodnitz was the first to leave Germany. In the late 1920s, after he lost his job at a German bank, he moved to New York and found a job on Wall Street. After a successful start, Otto was caught up in the upheaval that followed the Crash of October 1929. During the following years, until the United States entered World War II, Otto subsisted, working in less than stellar positions.

Their youngest son, Heinz, was an engineer. In the fall of 1929 (several years before the Nazis came to power) he was employed by the large German manufacturer I. G. Farben. When Heinz took a vacation day in celebration of Yom Kippur, his employer realized that he was Jewish and promptly fired him. Luckily, Heinz found a good position at a small factory in the town of Neisse, Germany (today, Nysa, Poland), where he stayed until the Nazis came to power. Shortly thereafter, in early 1933, the Nazi government confiscated the factory because it had a Jewish owner and fired all Jewish employees. Heinz and his recently wedded wife, Susi, moved back to Berlin. After realizing that they had no future in Nazi Germany, Heinz left the country for good in November 1933. Susi, who had to interrupt her studies when her advisor left Germany in mid-1933 for a position at Dartmouth College, followed Heinz to Palestine in early 1934.

Julius died in Berlin in 1936 when he was hit by a car. Grandma Hedwig left Germany shortly after Julius' death. She went first to the United States to visit her middle son, Otto, in New York City. Upon returning to Germany, Hedwig liquidated her apartment in Berlin and immigrated to Palestine to reside near Heinz and his family in Tel Aviv.

Three items that shed some light on Julius and Hedwig's activities in the years that followed the completion of the *Memories* appear in the epilogue and appendixes A and B.

The epilogue describes the events of the last years of Julius and Hedwig's lives. Also included are excerpts from Julius' diaries through 1936.

Appendix A is a translation of a speech that Julius delivered during the election campaign for the German Reichstag in August 1930.

Appendix B contains the translation of the lengthy notes that Julius dictated to Hedwig on April 28, 1934, while they were visiting Amsterdam. The write-up summarizes the events that took place in Germany and especially within the C.V. (*Der Centralverein deutscher Staatsburger Judischen Glaubens*) during those troubled days.

—Michael Brodnitz

Publisher's note: Michael's annotations appear in bracketed italics in the text.

Chapter 1
Julie Badt Herzfeld

Julie wrote this memoir in 1907.

Julie Badt Herzfeld as a young adult, likely in the 1870s

The Story of My Life, Put Together for My Children

MY FATHER, DAVID BADT (1808–1883) was born in Schwersenz [*then in Germany, now Swarzedz, Poland, 8 km east of Posen (or "Poznan" in Polish)*] on the day before Sukkot in 1808 [*October 5, 1808*], the son of Leib Jehuda (?–1816) and Leie (Lenchen) Badt (?–1813). The grandparents owned a wholesale business for manufactured products. They were part of the patrician Jewish families, the so-called *Yichus*, of the town. These [*the Yichus*] were the families whose forefathers had proven themselves worthy of this recognition, through their study of Talmud and Torah as well as by their charity.

When my father was five years old, his mother died. He then had a stepmother. When he was in his eighth year, his father died.

While it was assumed by the people in town that a significant fortune was left behind, it turned out that nothing was left. The relatives claimed that the stepmother took the whole inheritance. My father then became the responsibility of his uncle Abraham Badt, who was also a scholar. This uncle was very pleased with him because he learned easily and had good mental capacity.

Following his Bar Mitzvah at the age of thirteen, my father went, according to the traditions of the time, to study with famous Rabbis as a *Bocher* (student of Talmud). Places where fifty or more *Bochurim* congregated were called a *Yeshiva*. Father went at first to Rabbi Akiba Eger in Posen and then to the town of Graetz. As most of these young people were not blessed with fortunes, it was the tradition that the members of the Jewish congregation, who were better off, provide free meals and occasionally, room and board for these students. My father had three such regular places to dine free, for Saturday and two weekdays. For the rest of the week, he managed to get along on the support of his older brother, Israel, who provided him with one and one half Deutschmark (three Polish Gulden) per month. It is easy to appreciate that this only allowed for a minimal diet. As my father sometimes told us, during the remaining four days of the week when he had to feed himself, the money only allowed him to get two pieces of dry bread rolls, made of dark flour, at the cost of three Fens per day [*0.03 Deutschmark; one Fen or "Pfennig" was 0.01 Deutschmark*].

At the age of seventeen, my father, together with his somewhat older brother Jizchak, decided to go west [*to a part of Germany*] then known as Aschkenas, to become teachers. For this purpose, he passed the examination as a ritual butcher and got the certificate to that effect, which was attested to by three Rabbis. They traveled on foot to Detmold, and my father then got a teaching job in Lemgo [*both towns are in Germany, not far from Hannover*].

This position also allowed him to pursue German studies, which were at that time generally neglected. He studied on his own and did so with great energy. At the same time, he also learned French and Mathematics. All along, he also continued his studies of the Talmud.

After ten years, probably because he was tired of the life of an employee, my father returned to his hometown. There he became a businessman and participated with his elder brother Israel in enterprises in the town of Sagen in the area of Priebus. He got married in February of 1836.

My mother, whose name was Zerel (1813–1898), was the fourth daughter of Abraham and Roscher Levy (maiden name Badt). She was born two days after Yom Kippur, 1813 [*October 6, 1813*]. Her father was known under the name Reb Awrohom Wallner. For many years he operated a brewery and a distillery under lease from a Baron or Nobleman. Following the death of my grandmother in Obersitzko, my grandfather moved back to Rogasen, along with my mother and her younger sister. There he was considered a rather wealthy man. When my mother got married, he provided her with a dowry of one thousand Talers [*a silver coin struck in Austria with the image of Empress Maria Theresa, widely accepted in other countries as well*], which was considered at the time to be a rather substantial amount of money.

As the family of my grandfather considered itself as *Yichus* [*upper class*], Grandfather searched for a son-in-law with a similar *Yichus* background. Above all else, he was looking for someone with a good background in the studies of Talmud and Torah. Chaya, his eldest daughter, was married to a well-regarded man by the name of Landsberg who came from one of the foremost families.

A business that he tried in Rogasen failed, and he therefore accepted the post of a local Rabbi. A few years later he was summoned to serve as the Rabbi of the renowned community of

Zuelz [*now called "Biala II," 92 km south-southeast of Wroclaw*] in the district of Oberschlesien.

The second daughter, Bluemchen, married the well-known Talmud student Mr. Moses Herzfeld, who lived in the city of Graetz. They later became my parents-in-law.

The third daughter, Pesse, married a Mr. Fabisch Meyer from Wongrowitz [*Wagrowiec, 45 km north-northeast of Posen*]. A few weeks before my mother's wedding, my grandfather died. Both my mother and her younger sister Beile were accommodated by their in-laws, the Landsbergs. After their wedding, which took place three months later, my parents moved to Sagen in the district of Priebus. After one year, the cooperation of the two brothers was dissolved. The cause in part was that there was not enough to keep both brothers busy. The fact that the two women could not agree was also responsible for this parting.

My mother wanted to become more active in the business and therefore pushed for the separation. In the process, my parents lost about one half of the dowry. With the balance, they moved to a village by the name of Graefenhain that was three hours away. This village had a population of about one thousand residents and had both a Catholic and an Evangelic church. In that village they rented an apartment from which they ran a small business selling things that came from the Colonies and various other items. On Sundays, people from miles around would come to attend the churches. While there, they also went shopping in town and at its only store, which belonged to my parents.

Through their honesty and friendly conduct, my parents quickly acquired regular customers from among the farmers in the area, who also came to the clever Jew for advice regarding their difficult questions. Their wives came to talk over their problems with my mother, who was always friendly and who was also able to comfort them. On weekdays, while the farmers were busy in their fields, the store was very quiet. So my father started traveling with his merchandise to neighboring villages, thereby increasing the turnover of the business.

The first child, my brother Louis, was born in October 1837 (1837–1916). A *mohel* [*the person who performs a circumcision ceremony*] for the circumcision had to be brought from Glogau, which was twelve miles away. It was also difficult to get together the ten men needed for the *minyan* [*a group of at least ten men required by Jewish law to perform a religious group service*] as only a few Jews were living in the surrounding area. The nearest city was Sorau, three hours away, and it had only two Jewish families, which at that time and until 1847 was the legal limit on the number of Jewish residents that were allowed for that town [*in other words, by law, only two Jewish families were allowed to reside in many of these towns before 1847*]. These Jews, and the few others who resided in the surrounding areas, would get together during the High Holidays to form the group of ten men needed to carry out a community service.

My father, who was a much-acknowledged Talmud student, was the leader in the community prayers. He led the services, read the prescribed Torah portions and blew the *Shofar* [*ram's horn*]. For the Day of Atonement [*Yom Kippur*], an assistant prayer leader was engaged. For this occasion, my parents traveled a number of days before the holiday to Sorau. Only the Jewish maid stayed behind. In later years, when more children joined the family, the younger ones were also left behind. Mother, who wanted to be present when the services began at six in the morning, got up early in order to precook the midday meal. Breakfast was eaten before daybreak. In the evening, after the end of the holiday, my parents rode back to their home. One can only imagine how much my religious parents suffered from the separation from a Jewish community with which they could share their Saturday nights and other holidays throughout the year.

Getting kosher meat was equally a problem. Although my father was a certified slaughterer, he could only do so in the fall, when the farmers would butcher animals for Christmas. He would then take part of the beef and smoke it in order to keep it for later use. During the summer months, meat was had only rarely. The farmers raised some geese for their feathers but they had only few other edible birds. The geese were slaughtered in the fall. So for weeks on end, we were left without eating any meat in our meals.

In general, the way of life of my parents was rather simple. Bread was baked at our home; always enough of it was baked to last for two to three weeks at a time. The days of baking were feast days for the children. Mother would roll dough on a baking sheet and add butter on top, and then she sprinkled sugar on it. This became our cake. During the summer and fall, she covered apples and pears with bread dough and baked them for us, the children. There was no bakery in our village. Fresh breadcrumbs, for sale in the store on Sundays, were brought from a bakery in a village that was one and a half hours away. If at the end of the market day, any of these crumbs were left over, the children would get a portion of them during the following week. When the bread became too tough, our mother would toast it for us on the open fire. In total, the children were not spoiled. The upbringing of the children and the whole way of life were rather Spartan.

By and by the household became rich with children. In 1840 a sister, Roeschen, was born, followed by brothers Abraham in 1842 and Isidor in 1845, sister Lottchen in 1846, and myself on November 25, 1848. My brother Nathan followed in 1851, and my sisters Eugenie [*Jenny*] and Henriette [*Jettchen*] were born in 1853 and 1856, respectively. With the exception of the last two, all of the children were born in the so-called *Pottery,* which my parents had rented [*this was Julie's term for a place that had been acquired by her father and was formerly used to make clay pots*]. A few years ago Uncle Badt gave me a framed picture of this house for my birthday.

My parents often told me that I had been an early walker. Then I fell at one time and hurt myself severely. After that, I refused to walk or move on my own for a lengthy period of time. I do recall, however that once I dared to stand up and I walked throughout the house calling, "Open the door, I walked by myself."

Soon thereafter, my parents purchased a property adjacent to the Evangelic church, which included a big garden and a forge. We moved to this place, which by comparison with today's living places was rather modest. We felt that it was much more comfortable and the rooms were much larger than those that we had before. We were very satisfied and lucky in this place. The large yard was our special pleasure. In the summer, when fruit began to ripen on the trees, my brother Isidor and I could not wait and would be the first ones out to collect the fruit that had dropped from the trees.

My parents leased the forge and a small part of the garden. They also obtained two cows that were housed in an existing steel structure that was on the property. The milk and butter from these cows was partially sold by our parents.

In the large garden, a portion was cultivated with rye and potatoes. A meadow provided grass to feed the cows during the summer and hay for the winter. My mother cultivated the vegetable garden by herself. She grew all sorts of vegetables and salad greens, etc. The household not only used this produce but also offered it for sale. The children, under mother's supervision, did the weeding and raking. Because we were also allowed to participate in the planting of the flowers and their cultivation, we regarded it as a pleasure.

Once they had moved to the new, larger, and better salesrooms, my parents' business also improved. Consequently, our father could now concentrate all of his efforts solely on his purchasing activities. That too was not as simple in those days as it is today. At that time, one had to travel by horse and a cart to the fair that took place at Frankfurt a/O [*Frankfurt aan der Oder, a major city in the eastern part of Germany; the fair took place once a year*]. One had to plan one's purchases so that they would cover the needs of the business from one fair until the next. Then, with a loaded cart and over poor roads, one had to return home, often walking on foot beside the cart, over the course of several days. Only exceedingly limited and poor care and provisions were available along the way in those days. As a result of these strains on the health of Father, this once big and strong man had already suffered from poor health by the time he reached the age of 40. He never fully recovered again.

In order to benefit from a better school, my brother Louis was sent as a youngster to live with Uncle Landsberg in the town of Zuelz. My brother Isidor followed later to Sorau, where he was placed at the home of a Mr. Mendelsohn, an official of the Religious Authority. My sister Roeschen attended the Evangelic Village School in Graefenhain. I too started attending that school at the age of five. Father provided us with Hebrew and religious instruction. Abraham and Lottchen died while still young children. Choirmaster Krause had a daughter who was my age. The two of us competed constantly for the first place at school.

By the time I was eight years old, I had finished learning the complete curriculum of that school. At that time my brothers, Isidor, who stayed at the house of Mendelsohn in Sorau, and Nathan, who was not yet of school age and lived with my parents in Graefenhain, became seriously ill. The fact that it took a three-hour-long trip to fetch a doctor or medication may have contributed to the fact that Nathan did not survive the illness, while Isidor [*who was living in Sorau*] survived the crisis, just as his brother was buried.

These events probably caused our parents to decide to start a branch of the business in Sorau, which also allowed the younger children to attend a better school. My brother Louis, who was eleven years older than I, had by that time completed his apprentice period trading in sundry items in the town of Glogau. He was considered capable enough to oversee the new affiliate. My father purchased a house in Sorau and established the business in it. Isidor left the house of Mendelsohn, and we formed a household with our sister Roeschen, who supervised the place. Generally, our father stayed in Sorau from Tuesday through Friday. On Fridays he traveled to Mother, in Graefenhain, in order to spend the Saturdays with her and be there to help her on the main business day, which was on Sunday.

Naturally, the move also brought about some unpleasant results. Brother Louis became the master of the house and he set down some tough rules. Isidor tried to buck these rules. For me too, the brotherly rules were not always to my liking. For example, he ordered me to knit each day a piece of material that was twice the length of my brother's large hand, in addition to doing my school and house work. This often caused tears to run from my eyes. My brother knew how to get his orders fulfilled, and therefore I did not get the chance that my classmates had to take a walk after school. This pleasure was reserved only for Saturdays, when the business was closed and handwork was strictly forbidden. Sunday was the main business day, and all of us had to help out in the business to the extent that we were possibly able to do so.

I was admitted to the third grade at school. After half a year, I was promoted to the second level. At that time our family was hit by serious bad luck. Sister Roeschen became very ill while at the Ruhr River and died [*at age 19*]. At that time she was helping our mother in Graefenhain, offering great help in running the house and the business. She was only nineteen years old, and we were all saddened by this. She was always loving and kind to us, her younger siblings.

Upon learning of the loss, my mother's brother, Uncle Samuel Levy, who lived in Nakel, sent his son Jacob to live with and help mother during this difficult time at home and in the business. After about one year he left, and our parents took in the daughter of another Uncle Levy, who also lived in Nakel. This niece, who came from a household that was rather depressed, caused our mother some grief. Although mother was always active and busy, she could not manage to get the niece to carry out her share of the work.

Shortly after the death of our sister, my brother Louis was drafted to the army. Father was successful in getting him stationed in Sorau. It was customary at that time to have soldiers billeted at home. As a result, he was able to spend his admittedly limited free time helping in the business. By that time my brother Isidor was fourteen years old and he had very limited interest in studying. As he refused to study Greek, our father took him out of school after the seventh grade and employed him in the business. One can imagine how this business was if a fourteen-year-old fellow and, after school hours, a ten-year-old girl were able to run it. The location of the property that our father had purchased in Sorau was also not very suitable for a store.

At that time a very rare thing occurred when both of my mother's older sisters came together for a visit. Aunt Landsberg from Nicolai and Aunt Herzfeld from Graetz [*part of Germany at that time, currently in Poland and called Grodzisk*] came for their first visit to my parents. They stopped for a day with us in Sorau and then traveled to our mother in Graefenhain. On the day of their visit I had the bad luck that the handwriting teacher ordained a punishment period for me because the letter "l" that I had written was not to his liking. We had handwriting classes on Tuesdays and Saturdays. My father had me excused from the Saturday class and the teacher was furious as he declared that one hour per week was not enough time to master good handwriting. He cooled his fury by assigning me a punishment, knowing that I would be most unhappy with this, as this was my first punishment.

I came home in tears, and the aunts asked at once what had happened to me. Aunt Herzfeld consoled me by assuring me that the dark-haired youngster that she had at home would be kept for me [*this refers to a brother of Abraham Herzfeld, whom her aunt was reserving for Julie for marriage*]. She did not guess at that time that she was actually going to save her older son for me. This son was serving at that time in Freystadt in Silesia [*Kozuhow near Nowa Sol, 119 km southwest of Posen*]. During the following year, he came for a visit while on his vacation. As he frequently told me later, he had already fallen for the little schoolgirl in the jacket with black and white squares. I too liked the cousin very much. No wonder, as he courted me and took me for walks, whereas my brothers never spoiled me in this regard.

As the school years came to an end, I was proud to have been among the top three students in my class. This was, in part, thanks to the ease with which I was able to learn. I competed with two of my classmates for the top place, and in my senior year I was given a very good report card. My sister Jenny had also come to Sorau in the meantime. Together we went for vacations to our mother in Graefenhain, where in the summer and fall, it was a special pleasure to be active in the garden.

Mother saw to it that one did not idle about. During the summer there was work to be done in the garden. Then we had to glue together bags, as at that time ready-made bags were not available. For each thousand pieces that we made, we got ten Fen, always rounded down to one hundred pieces. On top of this, the wash also had to be embroidered with a cross-stitched identification mark. We were given ten Fens for each four items, etc. These payments served as our pocket money for the school year. On busy days at the store, I had to help in the business. I was also given the responsibility for the sale of toys and the Christmas cakes during the Christmas holidays.

To this end, I asked to be excused from school one week before the end of the term, in the Christmas period during the last two years of my school days. This coincided with the busiest period in the store. As I was a good student, these requests were granted.

During my last school year, the hardware store that was located next to the marketplace was offered to my father. He took over the store. By then my brother Louis had completed his military service and was able to help in running the store. As the turnover of the business increased within a short period of time, my parents decided to sell the store in Graefenhain and reunite the family. Within a short time they found a solid buyer, and in January 1863, my mother and sister Jettchen [*Henriette*] joined us. We took residence in an apartment in the same house.

By then I had graduated from school and so I was given the responsibility for maintaining the house. During Sundays and on market days, I had to be in the store. So as to not neglect the household work, I had to get up very early on those days. I therefore had to get up at four in the morning on Fridays during the months of November and December in order to prepare the meals for Saturday's lunch and Friday's dinner by nine on Friday. Starting at nine in the morning, I had to be ready to serve in the store. In order to be able to do this, all preparations had to be completed by Thursday afternoon. I frequently was extremely frozen in the cold kitchen. Once I wanted to make it easier on myself. I made all the preparations on the Thursday. After Mother woke me up at four a.m. I let the helping maid get up by herself and start the fire. Mother came back to check, about one and a half hours later, which never happened before. When she saw that the maid was sitting alone in front of the boiling pot of meat, she created such a scene that I never dared to try and do this again.

That was how life went on at a steady pace. A very enjoyable change was the visit by mother's younger sister, Aunt Koenisberg from Rogasen, who came with Cousin Nettchen from Graetz for a fourteen-day-long visit. Cousin Nettchen had gone to her sister Ernestine's place, where she had taken care of her sister during the first weeks, while she was confined to bed. She stopped on the way back to Graetz for a visit at her aunt's place at nearby Rogasen. She then came with her to Sorau. This visit had an important influence on the future of my brother Louis.

During the fall of 1864, cousins Jettchen [*Henriette, born Herzfeld*] and Bertchen Herzfeld got married at the same time in Graetz. Louis and I were supposed to attend the double wedding. Suddenly, events at the business prevented us from going on this trip, which I had anticipated with joy.

In February of 1865, when I was sixteen years old, Cousin Abraham stopped by on the return trip from Berlin. He suggested to my parents that I travel with him to Graetz, as I could not come to the weddings. Father approved my going and my mother, although reluctantly, allowed me to go. This trip was a major event for me, especially as it was the first trip of my life. We arrived in Graetz after a difficult trip, which included a half-day stop at Lissa [*Leszno*], where my cousin [*Abraham*] had business with a factory that made glue for roofing, while I visited a relative. In Graetz I was received by my relatives with love. I soon became close with Cousin Nettchen [*Julie's sister-in-law*], and her friends, and both cousins accepted me with love.

One can imagine that this had a great impact on me. Whereas at home I was glued to a treadmill, I found here, among the relatives, kindness and openness. I was treated and accepted as a grown up young lady by my local cousins Roeschen and Jettchen [*Henriette*] and their husbands. No wonder that I liked it all very much.

I had a three-week-long vacation. Toward the end of that period, a dance was scheduled for a place named "The Resource," and my parents allowed me to take part in it. In the meantime, I was expected to visit Aunt Koenisberg in Rogasen. To make sure that I followed the plan, my parents sent the material and trimmings for a ball gown to Rogasen, where I was supposed to have it fitted for me.

The visit with the childless elder relatives was not too interesting. Uncle did not pay much attention to me, as he spent the days with his card-playing friends. My aunt had enough to do in taking care of my uncle's needs, in addition to the business. I, therefore, stayed there just long enough to have my ball dress made and then traveled back to Graetz. I had to pass through Posen, where I visited a cousin, and then traveled through the night to Graetz. This whole trip had to be done via a postal cart, which accounts for the length of time it took to complete this journey. Nowadays, one could travel all the way to Basel [*in Switzerland*] in a similar period of time.

In the meantime, everything in Graetz was prepared for the ball. We had a great time during the dance. In addition to my two cousins, a number of young people were also present at the ball. I danced rather frequently on this, my first such event and have looked back on this evening with great pleasure. All too soon, the date of my departure for my home, which was set by my parents, came about. Within a couple of days of that date, Cousin Bernhard Stern was scheduled to travel to Breslau to go shopping for the business. He had ordered a direct cart to take him from Graetz to the train station in Altboyn. My relatives talked me into staying a few additional days in Graetz and then to travel to Lissa under his protection. When I came home my father welcomed me, saying they were considering sending me some funds so I could rent a small place in Graetz. I have long recalled this trip with pleasure.

On April 1, 1865, my brother Isidor started his year of military service in Sorau. He was getting prepared for so-called "press service." As he had been billeted at home, this caused some disruptions in the household. On the day before he was due to be released, an order was issued to retain all those who were enlisted. Shortly after that there was a general mobilization of reservists and the war with Austria, in which my brother was involved [*this war between Austria and Germany is known as the Seven Weeks' War; following it, Austria was forced to give up its leadership in German politics*]. After that he had to stay as part of the occupation force in Saxony. My brother Louis was called up to serve in the reserves in July. He became part of the force that was sent to Posen. However, in the storeroom they could not locate a uniform that was big enough to fit him, and he had to walk around clad in his drill jacket. He was released again when a few days later, the battle of Koeniggraetz ended with success for the Prussians and peace was in sight.

Late in the fall of 1866, we were surprised by a visit from Uncle Herzfeld and Cousin Abraham. They had been on business to Frankfurt aan der Oder and on the way back they stopped for a visit. As I had mentioned earlier, such visits by relatives were rather rare and therefore were even more enjoyed when they occurred.

I was especially glad because, during my visit to Graetz, I had developed the highest respect and love for my Uncle and developed a special interest in my Cousin Abraham. Shortly after the visit we received notice that Cousin Nettchen became engaged to a Mr. Kalisch, who lived in the town of Schrimm. She [*Nettchen, Julie's sister-in-law*] had met him when she visited her married sister, who lived in Schrimm. My brother Louis was disappointed by the news, as he had developed an interest in her after her earlier visit to us. When he completed his military service in Posen during the summer, he traveled to Graetz on his way home, in the hope of speaking to her. This did not materialize as she was at that time in Schrimm, visiting her sister.

Early in February of 1867, I caught a bad cold, which developed into a serious lung infection. While I had normally been most active, my mother, who usually worked in the business, took over all the household responsibilities from me and she saw to it that I followed the Doctor's instructions and stayed out of the cold air and the wind. I was treated and cared for and within a few weeks, I made a good recovery.

One day at the beginning of March, Mother came to the living room in which Father was sitting while I was busy doing some handicraft. In her hand she carried a letter. Without sharing with me her excitement, she said, "Daddy, we have a *schiddach* [*a match*] for our Julchen, you'll never guess who it is." My father winked in my direction, and they both left for another room.

I was, of course, very curious as to who it might be. After a few days I learned from Father, with whom I was especially close, that Cousin Abraham, through his brother-in-law Breslauer, asked my parents whether or not they were inclined to have me get married. If so, he would like to come and ask for my hand. Before sending a reply, my father wanted to check first with the doctor as to whether or not my health allowed such a move. When the doctor gave a positive reply, father wanted to know how I felt about it. Considering the special feelings that I had for my cousin, it was very easy for me to give my consent. And so, my uncle and aunt Herzfeld and my cousin and his parents came to us in order to celebrate with us the engagement in the family circle. This took place on April 3, 1867.

Our engagement was a very happy time, although our visits during that period were rather sparse. That was a function of the times and the difficulties in travel of those days. During Whitsunday [*Pentecost*] he came again and spent eight days with us. My dear parents saw to it that we could enjoy longer periods without disruption, which made up for the long waiting time.

We then proceeded in putting together my trousseau [*a trunk with which a bride in those days might be sent off with her silver, ceramics, etc.*]. When my sister Jenny finished school on the first of April 1867, she dedicated herself to carrying out my responsibilities in

Early picture of Abraham Herzfeld, husband of Julie Badt Herzfeld, likely in the 1870s

running the household. In July my father and I went to Salzbrunn. I went in part to accompany my father and in part to get over the remaining inflammation of my respiratory tract. After a stay of four weeks, the doctor told us: "You can get married now; everything is in the best of order."

On our trip back, we stayed for a few days in Breslau, where several of Uncle Landsberg's children were living. Cousin Ferdinand was a student at that time. He dedicated his full time to showing us all the sites in Breslau. We visited everything that was worth seeing, including even the reptile collection at the local university.

In August, at the special request of my future in-laws, we visited Graetz where my groom awaited me. My brother Isidor accompanied us during this stay.

The wedding day was then set for October 30, 1867. At the request of my in-laws, the location was moved to Posen. Uncle Landsberg, who was a Rabbi in the town of Nicolai, performed the marriage ceremony. I had never before attended a Jewish wedding. The impressive appearance of my uncle, his nice wedding speech, and the whole dignified ceremony left a very deep impression on me. From among my siblings, only my brother Louis was present, as Isidor and my two sisters were left at home in order to take care of the business and the household. The household was rather larger at that time, as it included four young people who were staying with our parents for room and board. A sister of my father, Aunt Jossmann from Schwersenz, took care of all the preparations for the wedding. She took good care of everything, and all the guests were very satisfied.

There was no time for a wedding shower as the day before the wedding, Tuesday, October 29, was the annual market day in Graetz. The groom and my future mother-in-law could not leave Graetz before five in the afternoon. Even though they hired a special horse and carriage to make the trip, they arrived in Posen only at ten in the evening. My father and sister-in-law Stern only arrived in Posen at noon of the actual wedding day. Other siblings, who were residing in Graetz, could also not attend as they had to take care of the business and the household. Everyone stayed at the Hotel Keilers, where both the actual ceremony and wedding meal took place.

On Thursday, the day after the wedding, we traveled to Graetz. Father also came with us. Mother and Louis traveled directly back to Sorau. We arrived rather late in the day and found that our apartment was nicely appointed. I had known the place from my earlier visit and felt like a queen in my own place. The place created a wonderful impression with its plush sofa, two leather armchairs, six chairs, and a magnificent velour carpet. The shining floor of the hallway was also remarkable. In contrast with these appearances, the atmosphere in the house was not a joyful one, especially considering that a young couple was moving in.

My brother-in-law Meschulem was expected to report for military service on the following Saturday, while my sister-in-law Jeanette, whom I had remembered as an easygoing and happy young lady, was now changed and very quiet.

On Friday we went to the civil marriage, accompanied by both fathers. This act took place, at that time, only after the religious wedding. On Saturday morning a big presentation took place at the synagogue. Following religious services I was introduced to the old Rabbi Guttmacher, who lived in the *Bethhamidrasch* [*the school*] next to the synagogue. It was the tradition since time immemorial that the Rabbi had a talk with each young woman. Of course, the whole congregation stood in front of the place, to see and review critically the young Mrs. Herzfeld and what she had brought with her. The way I looked at it, this amounted to having to run the gauntlet, which one could not avoid. That afternoon, all those who considered themselves to be friends or acquaintances came to the apartment to congratulate us and, what was probably more important, to have a chance to see the young wife and the new apartment.

On Sunday Father left us, and at the same time my husband had to leave on a business trip. They shared a wagon until they reached the town of Kosten. I used the afternoon to put my things away. My sister-in-law Nettchen was much help with that. In the course of this activity, we became closer again and I learned that her engagement with Kalisch had been annulled. It turned out that both his personality and his financial circumstances were misrepresented. So far, however, no one talked about this in public. This explained why the household appeared under pressure. This conversation was a big relief for my sister-in-law.

We decided to keep house jointly with my in-laws. I wanted to get integrated into the business as my sister-in-law was staying in the house. She introduced me into both the business as well as the household. I quickly realized that there was not much that I could do in the business without learning Polish. As soon as my husband returned from his business trip, he hired a Polish teacher for me. The teacher came to our home four hours each week. I studied with him for one hour each Monday, Tuesday, Wednesday, and Thursday. He gave me assignments of vocabulary and passages to translate. It gave me, as well as my able teacher, great satisfaction when after a few hours I was able to make myself understood by both my teacher as well as the people in the business.

In the meantime Christmas came, which brought with it a visit by my brother Louis. He had heard about the dissolved engagement of my sister-in-law, which by now had become known. He wanted to try to see whether or not [*Nettchen*], for whom he had long ago developed an interest, would consent to his approach. She agreed with pleasure, and the senior Herzfelds were also very pleased with this turn of events, not less so than the elder Badts, who greeted this daughter-in-law with happiness.

The official engagement took place during the month of February. My dear father came to that event. My brother Louis stayed with us during the Easter holidays, and the wedding was set for the Whitsunday week. Let me just add that in spite of the intensive daily activities, we also managed to have an active social life. The resources provided by my dear husband permitted us to have, every fourth Saturday night, a coffee *klatch* [*circle*], which included the performance of a few one-act plays. My dear husband usually took upon himself one of the leading acting roles. Therefore, the rehearsals usually were held in our place, which gave rise to many varied activities. After the efforts of the day we were glad to have these enjoyable evenings. When Saturday evening of the performance came, one had to prepare and make kosher the four geese, which were purchased on the previous Friday, and quickly change and get ready to go to the plays.

I had very good relations with my parents-in-law and my sister-in-law, Nettchen. Although there were some differences of opinion between us about the running of the common household, these never resulted in any serious misunderstandings.

Because of the frequent business trips of my husband, having this common household was actually rather pleasant, as I would otherwise have had to be alone very often. We divided the responsibilities in such a way that during the week in which sister-in-law Nettchen supervised the business, I took care of the household. During the following week, when I spent my time minding the business, she took care of the household.

In May, Nettchen and I went together for a multiday trip to shop for the items that were needed for her dowry. To go to Posen one had to travel via the postal or some other cart. Neither was a very pleasant way to travel. The wedding took place a few days after Whitsunday. Mother came to us for her first visit. My father and sister Jettchen [*Henriette*], who was twelve years old at that time, came to accompany her while Isidor and Jenny stayed behind to mind the house and the business. Uncle Landsberg gave the wedding speech while Rabbi Guttmacher of Graetz performed the service. He did so in the open in the yard of Hotel Kutznerchen. He only trusted the open skies. I enjoyed this ceremony, but my parents did not find this open-air service to their liking.

The young couple, accompanied by my parents and sister, left on the following day. We had made up in advance that in early July we would go together on a so-called honeymoon trip to the mountains of *Schlesien* [*Silesia*].

The next few weeks passed in redoubled activity. My brother-in-law Breslauer from Schrimm, who felt very obliged to my husband for his help in getting his business started, announced that he would take over my husband's place in the business for the duration of our trip. We ordered a couple of carts to take us to Kosten, which had, at that time, the nearest railroad station.

We departed by an open cart at two in the morning. We were in the middle of the four-miles-long trip when a fierce storm broke out and forced us to stop at a village coffee stop.

With some effort, we reached the station at six in the morning and traveled by train to Sorau where we arrived at noon. At our parent's house we enjoyed a good midday meal, and at two in the afternoon we continued our trip in the direction of Dresden, together with my brother Louis and wife, Nettchen. We stopped on the way in Goerlitz, where a friend of my husband, from the time of their military service, was living.

We arrived in Dresden completely exhausted at eleven at night. We stayed there for three days, viewing the art treasures of the museum, the beautiful locations in the city, as well as the wonderful surrounding areas. One night we went to the opera house, where a wonderful performance of Rienzi took place. All these impressions left a deep mark on me. Both of us women felt that we were lucky beggars to have had the opportunity to get to see such wonderful sites. On the other two evenings, we went to a terrace with a great view and to a charming small village. On the fourth day we traveled by a steamboat to Wehlen, from where we hiked to the bastion. From there we traveled by steamer to Koenigstein. This was followed by a hike to and from the old fortifications, and then we sailed by steamer to Schandau, where we landed and stayed in a town named Sending.

A cool dip in the river Elbe felt good after a hot day of achievements. Early on the next morning, we left by carriage to Kuhstall. From there we walked and then rode on a horse to the large and to the small Winterberge [*in Switzerland*] where, as has often been told, our horses just kept on going [*this last phrase appears to be an idiomatic expression*].

We went back down to Hernskretschen and continued by steamer to Aussig. We arrived rather late and therefore had to book a hotel-steamship room. We could, however, not use the beds because they were full of bugs. Instead we lay down on the carpet, where we could not sleep, but at least we rested. The following morning we went to Töplitz, where we viewed the baths, the spa, and the walkways. We also went to Schlossberg [*in Germany, I believe*]. In the afternoon we traveled to Prague, where we wanted to spend Saturday and Sunday.

My brother Louis proved to be an excellent tour director who was very quick in discovering the main worthwhile attractions of each place. He led us to see the main sites. On Saturday morning we started by going to the Altenschul synagogue, where prayers were being held. The men went to the main section of the synagogue, while the ladies went to the ladies section. The weekly portion of the Torah was being read. This synagogue is well known as it is partially set under the street level. The women's section goes all around, separated by a heavy wall from the men's section. Both sections are connected by openings with small windows, which are shaped with an arch at their top. One can hear the sound of the prayer, but only the ladies who were seated near the door could see or understand the leader of the services. We followed this visit by a stop at a newer synagogue, where the ritual was similar to the one that we were used to from home, although this location was decorated with unusually pretty curtains and other hangings.

Next we went to see the Market with the Apostles' Clock, where all figures appeared in a row at precisely twelve o'clock. We also visited the church of St. Nepomuk (with its forty heavy, silver-coated sarcophagi and its chapel, which is decorated with Bohemian precious stones) as well as many other worthwhile sites. Then we went to eat. While traveling through the mountains, we made up for the lack of kosher food in those sites by eating eggs and similar items. In Teplitz and Prague we found some most enjoyable dishes. We had fun learning to identify previously unknown dishes, which were very tasty. That afternoon, we visited the *Hradschin* [*the Castle District in Prague*] with its many buildings and halls, in which much that was old and beautiful was displayed. On Sunday morning we visited the old Jewish cemetery, with its multitude of historic monuments. After that we viewed the business traffic in the Jewish part of the town, a place that was very silent on Saturday. In the afternoon we took a trip to Baumgarten [*in the Czech Republic*], which is a destination for many residents of

Prague, and then on to Reichenberg, where we were to begin our return trip.

My brother Louis handled the financial side of our trip. Whenever it was time, he asked my husband to help and share in the expenses. When he ran out of cash in Prague, it turned out that my husband had plenty of money but it was in the form of securities issued by someone in West Prussia, which no one in Prague wanted to exchange for local currency. The cash that Louis possessed was sufficient to cover the cost of the hotel bill, but it was not enough to pay for the trip to Reichenberg. So the wives emptied the change from their purses, and the total was just enough to pay for the ride to Reichenberg. It was, however, not enough to hire a cart from the train station to the hotel. We made it to the hotel after dark, on a rainy evening. We had planned to get some money by telegraph-transfer from Sorau. However, a banker in Reichenberg did cash some of the securities, and we could proceed with our travel to Sorau in good spirits. This whole affair resulted in a lot of fun even when we had to buy tickets in the far back rows at a concert in Baumgarten, which was all we could afford at the time.

My dear husband traveled back home at once, while Louis, Nettchen, and I went to Sorau, where I stayed at my parents' house for a few days. I have reminisced about this nice trip for many years. Often these stories came up when my siblings got together.

Five months later, on December 24, 1868, our first child, a solid and healthy boy, was born. We welcomed our good luck, as did the parents on both sides of the family. As soon as my mother received the telegraphic news, she rushed to be with us. My father came to the *brit,* which took place December 31, 1868. The physician did not approve of my plans to breast-feed the baby. Instead, we had to engage a wet nurse. The child Max, or with the Jewish name Meschulem (1868–1872), was named after the father of my father-in-law. He flourished and was a pleasure for the whole household. Grandfather Herzfeld [*likely Moses Herzfeld, father of my father-in-law*], who was a friend of all children, took much time to care for the little one.

About one year later, on December 13, 1869, a second young son was born. He was named Louis (1869–1870) (Leib, after my father's father). Because of the Christmas season's business, my mother could not come this time. Instead, my sister-in-law Jettchen Stern came from Schrimm to take care of the household and me. Live-in help did not exist in those days, and both my mother-in-law and father-in-law were weak and, therefore, required help for themselves.

This time, I was able to breast-feed the baby by myself. This was not without some problems, and, therefore, we had to add the help of a bottle. This child too was good, and it was a pleasure to have these two good-looking youngsters. I wished to share my pleasure with my parents and, therefore, on Whitsunday 1870, I traveled with both children to Sorau. This resulted in much joy for all concerned.

In the fall of 1869, my brother-in-law Meschulem completed his military obligations. He became active in the metal business and roofing factory, while my completely exhausted husband, together with the old Mr. Gutsche, were very busy setting up a brick factory. Shortly after we got married, my father-in-law took my husband as a partner in both the metal business and in the roofing factory. The brick factory was, however, run separately in partnership with Gutsche.

Upon our return from Sorau, we heard the news from Ems [*this telegram, known as the "Ems Dispatch," caused France to declare war on Prussia in the War of 1870*]. Both my brother-in-law [*Meschulem*] and my brother Isidor [*also referred to as "Uncle Isidor Badt"*] were called up at once and both participated in the campaign. Our family doctor Dr. Litthauer had to go and serve as a physician in the army, leaving in Graetz only Dr. Cohn, who was busy from morning until night, helping in the birth of newborn babies.

All at once, our youngest son became ill. We could only reach the doctor on the evening of the second day. Although everything that was available at the time was tried, and the boy was covered with compresses, the catastrophe hit on the third day, and the child died from the infection on August 18 [*1870*].

Our pain was great, and the grandparents mourned with us. On top of this, we were subject to the awful daily news from the front, where my brothers were in constant danger.

The news of victory, which brought joy to the whole world, did not help us, as it did not bring back our darling, who was lost to us in the first place because of the events of the war.

Months of silent suffering followed. Uncle Herzfeld was stationed outside Paris where, because of frequent minor attacks and because of poor care, he suffered much. Uncle Isidor Badt [*Julie's brother*] belonged to a unit that was part of the siege of the city Metz. He was then transferred to the Loire Army and returned from France in the winter. Uncle Herzfeld was assigned to a unit that stayed in France because of Alsace-Lorraine [*currently a part of France, this region had been annexed by Prussia in the War of 1870*]. He returned home to Graetz on June 10, 1871, and, on June 12, our dear daughter Rosa [*1871–1932*] was born.

I did not consent to having her fed by anyone else. After the first few weeks, in which she was a small crybaby, she became a quiet and brave little one so that one hardly knew that she was in the house. At given times she was picked up and fed. The rest of the time, when she was not sleeping, she lay happily in her cart so that one had a lot of pleasure from her.

Naturally, because of the experience with the loss of the other child, even more care was showered on this little one. Even though I had much to do in the business, the fact that the apartment was so near to the business made it possible for me to take care of both children with ease.

Little Max was a pretty, strong, and extremely bright young boy, full of life and energy. He had a playmate in his cousin Max Stern, who was older by three and one half weeks. The two boys played often together. The nursery maid, whom we engaged, could not handle both children. As I was unable to spend the whole day with the children, we sent him in April 1872 to Miss Krausse's kindergarten. Within a short time, the three-and-one-half-year-old boy was able to write as well as one would expect, nowadays, of a seven-year-old boy. We did not wish this, but that was the way kindergartens were run in those days. The boy did not enjoy going there but was reconciled to it by the fact that other boys of similar age were also there.

In the evening of June 27, 1872, our boy went to bed healthy and happy. At three in the morning, he came to our adjacent bedroom and rested next to his beloved father. He then went back to his bed without a word. At five a.m. he suddenly screamed a few times. We rushed to his room and found that he was strangely sick. We assumed it was a browning [*an inflammation of the tonsils*], which was rather common at that time. While I applied compresses on his little neck, my husband rushed to fetch the doctor, who soon arrived. Although the doctor made a valiant effort and provided some medication and we followed all his instructions, the boy was dead by early afternoon. An inflammation of the brain caused the loss. It was a serious blow to lose the second wonderful child in such a way! My dear husband, who loved the youngster above all else, was inconsolable. We were able to bear this loss only because of the close cooperation between the two of us. The whole town shared in our mourning, as all loved the pretty and smart child.

The following day Rosa was one year old, according to the Jewish calendar, which was used at that time to mark birthdays. A sad birthday!

A few weeks later my brother Isidor married Regina Badt, who lived in Schwersenz. She was the daughter of a cousin of my father, and they were engaged in April. Because of the deep mourning over our child, we did not want to take part in the festivities. My mother-in-law traveled to the wedding and came back accompanied by Aunt Nettchen from Schwersenz. Our aunt stayed with us for a week. Upon pressure from my husband and my parents, I went with her to Sorau.

I did not want to separate from my child and therefore took her with me. The love of my parents and siblings did me a lot of good. After fourteen days, I traveled back to our home with my child.

The great pain caused by the loss was made milder with the passage of time, but neither of us could ever completely overcome these losses.

The following winter Father [*her husband*] suggested that I should accompany him on his annual purchasing trip for the roofing factory. This trip to Berlin was aimed at taking my mind off my pain and having me get to know the capital city.

We left our only child with a reliable young lady, under the supervision of my in-laws. Aunt Stern promised to look after the child frequently. My husband wanted to turn back after five days. I was encouraged to stay for a couple of additional days, with cousin Jossmann, who had invited me to stay with them. My cousin, his wife, and their eldest daughter, who was thirteen years old, spent the time with me in the kindest fashion. While my husband spent the day doing his work, we used the evenings to go to the theater or other enjoyable places (of which there was, at that time, a much smaller variety and number than there were in later days, or today). We also went to hear the opera *Mignon*, which I enjoyed very much. One evening the men took us to the ballroom Orpheum. I was disgusted by the behavior of those who were there and requested to leave the place, which we did.

Accompanied by the Joosmann family members, I visited the art collections in Berlin. When I recall all that I had seen six years earlier in Dresden, the Berlin collections seemed to me to be second best.

With the exception of the Jossmann family, we had only a few relatives in Berlin at that time so that this did not take much of our time there. Casper Levy, who had a responsible position with Firma Treitel, devoted a whole evening to us. We spent that evening in the company of his sister Lichtenstein. At the end of my stay, I took part in the engagement party for a niece of Jossmann.

On the return trip I had planned to stop for a day and visit with my parents in Sorau. I came to them unannounced, and the surprise was complete. After being away from home for twelve days, I traveled back. There I was unpleasantly surprised to find that Rosa had scarlet fever. My parents did worry very much about this but did not want to inform me of it, as they did not want me to cut the trip short. Fortunately, it was a light case and she soon recovered from it.

We planned to construct a building during the summer of 1873. My dear husband purchased the wine arbor that was across the street from our property where a small butcher's store and a small cottage were located. The town purchased both of these structures from us. They wanted to tear them down in order to widen the street and make it as wide as it is in front of the pharmacy. We were short of space for the business, especially for the storage of items that had to be purchased in bigger quantities. For this purpose, we had rented a small plaster structure on the Fleischerstrasse [*"Butchers' Street"*]. This place was no longer big enough for our needs, as the business had grown from year to year. We therefore built a storage building at the corner of the Fleischerstrasse that also included some rental apartments. On the

The old Herzfeld house and business, circa 1870

The Herzfeld house and business, enlarged and improved, circa 1880

other corner we built a shed and a basement for our own use. Business relations with our partner had become difficult in those days. Old man Gutsche, our partner in the roofing and brick factories, did not want to undertake these construction projects. My husband provided two skilled brick layers to Mr. Gutsche, and he was supposed to supervise their work. For this effort he was paid 10 percent of the labor charges. He did not pay much attention to the work, so my husband had to take care of the work by himself to make sure that all was done as it was supposed to be.

With the anticipated arrival of Lenchen, I was rather occupied. Whereas in previous pregnancies, all preceded rather uneventfully, I was suffering from an assortment of pains on this occasion. Nonetheless, I had to carry out my responsibilities up to the end.

The business was rather brisk at that time. We had to make deliveries for some new constructions in Wonsowo, and as a result, my husband and even Papa Herzfeld had to travel to Neutomischel for the delivery of such products. On top of that, the house was full of company for weeks on end. Rabbi Willner, whose wife was a sister of my father-in-law, came with their daughter for an extended stay with the brother, before they left for the United States. Sister-in-law Ernestine Bischofswerder also came with three children to spend a vacation with us. With good will, all worked out, but I was exhausted when the guests all left.

On September 21, *Erev* [*evening*] Rosh Hashanah, our Lenchen was born [*Lenchen is a nickname that was used for Julie's daughter, Helene (1873–?)*]. She was a skinny girl with dark hair. This was in contrast to the earlier children, who all came into the world with blond hair and light-colored skin. My mother sent to me a children's maid from Sorau named Helene Gersene. She was highly recommended and did indeed prove to be very good. My mother also sent my sister Jenny to help me with the household while the baby was still in the children's bed. The child developed slowly, and when Rosa came down with a cough in early January,

Jenny picked it up as well. In those days it was not yet the practice to isolate the healthy children from the sick ones.

More than once I had the great fear, when the little one was hot and became blue in the face from coughing. All the medications that were prescribed by the doctor did not have any real effect. In early May the doctor suggested that perhaps a change in the air would help. Trips to a spa, as they are done nowadays, were not common at that time, especially not with young children. Instead I went to the parents' place in Sorau. Neither the doctor nor my siblings in Sorau had any fear that their children would get infected, in spite of the fact that Rosa played with their children, Albert and Lenchen [*those were the children of Louis Badt and Nettchen Herzfeld*].

Very soon, our children recovered from the cough. After a three-week stay, we traveled back home with the children's maid. On that occasion, I was almost left behind in Bomst. At that time, they didn't yet have toilets on board the trains. I had need for such a facility and one was located across the station from our rail car, and so I rushed to it. However, by the time I came out, the train had already started moving. I decided at once to jump on the step with the intention to ride this way for the remaining of the fairly short journey to Bentschen. The children's maid as well as Rosa made so much fuss and were so excited, thinking that I was left behind, that it was assumed by the train's crew that something bad had happened. The driver stopped the train again and the conductor, who had learned by then what had happened, told me to move to the car in which the children were. The daring deed was probably not good for my health.

On arriving at home of course I told the whole tale. My dear husband was horrified by this youthful indiscretion, and my father-in-law declared, "The mess turned out well, but it still is a mess."

On February 14, 1875, another keeper of the Herzfeld name arrived, welcomed by the grandparents from both sides of the

Julie and Abraham Herzfeld, as a young couple, likely in the 1870s

family. For several weeks before and after the birth of Ernst Solomon, the weather was extremely cold. The so-called good room, which was normally kept closed, had to be heated for days before the *brit* [*the circumcision*], to make the room acceptable. My sister Jenny came again to help me and take care of preparations for the circumcision. Father did not let the cold weather keep him away from Graetz and was also present for the occasion. Unfortunately, the circumcision was followed by some excessive bleeding which, as one can imagine, caused some excitement. It took over one hour before the doctor was able to put an end to it. We had always attributed the excessive paleness that our son had until he went to high school in Posen to this loss of blood.

When Solomon, who later called himself Ernst, was half a year old, my sister Jenny got married in Sorau [*she married Simon Krombach; they had six children, one of whom was Goldi, the mother of Vera v.d. Walde who later married Kurt Behrend in Buenos Aires; Kurt was the brother of Susi Behrend, my mother, who married Heinz Brodnitz in 1931; as far as we can tell, this double connection of the families was a coincidence*].

I wanted to help Mother in the preparations and, therefore, weaned the child, whom I was again feeding by myself, and traveled eight days before the wedding to the parents' house with Rosa, who in the meantime was four years old. My husband arrived only for the wedding itself. Nettchen and I took care of the bulk of the preparations. A local cook, under the supervision of a Jewish woman, cooked the meals on the wedding day itself. Uncle Landsberg [*husband of Julie's aunt, Chaya*] came again and performed the marriage ceremony and celebrated with us the pleasant addition to the family. On the following day we left and traveled together with the young couple to Opalenitza. At that point we separated, with the new couple heading to their new home in Posen while we went to our home in Graetz. During the fall, brother-in-law [*brother of Abraham Herzfeld*] Meschulem, who established a roofing factory in Sorau, got married. At the request of my in-laws, I traveled with them and with sister-in-law Roeschen Stern to the wedding, which took place in Spandau.

In the following winter a lung infection reappeared. I had picked up a bad cold infection and our local doctor, Dr. Cohn, in my opinion, attributed too much meaning to it. At my mother's request, I consulted a specialist, [*another*] Dr. Cohn, in Posen, with whom we consulted in all special medical cases. When he learned that I was in other circumstances [*i.e., pregnant*], he ordered that, before all else, I should stop the breast-feeding. To make me stronger, he ordered salt-water baths. He also wanted me to get special care, which he did not think the resort baths would provide, as their food was not sufficiently nourishing.

He suggested that it would be best if someone related could help in my care. My parents requested that I come to them in Sorau, and mother undertook to help with the baths and all else that was necessary. In those days there were neither bathtubs nor showers in homes. Water was heated in a wash kettle. It then served as a tub. In a household in which there was good will, all was possible. My sister Jettchen, who ran the household, helped me with much love and care. The results of all this care and love were a clear success. I had put Rosa with the other two young children under the care of my parents, and a reliable children's maid stayed with me in the house. On Whitsunday my dear husband, as well as the young couple from Posen, came for a visit so that the Badt siblings got together again.

During the month of September of that year [1876], my parents retired from the business and decided to move to Posen where my father found all that he needed to live as an Orthodox Jew. They settled in the same building in which my sister Jenny was living. As they could move in only on October 1, they spent the month of September, during which the High Holidays fell, with us in Graetz, as did sister Jettchen as well.

A young girl whom we named Emma and whose Jewish name was Ester, arrived on September 6. Most disturbing was the fact that the child was born with her head compressed on one side. As soon as she could travel, we decided to see a specialist. We were informed that Professor Fisher, who lived in Breslau, would be coming to help the sick Dr. Bendowski. When we inquired, Dr. Fischer agreed to examine the child. Following the examination he told us that at that time nothing could be done. When the child reached the age of one and a half, we should bring her to him in Breslau and he would try to help her.

In the meantime, my parents moved to Posen and shortly thereafter, my in-laws retired from the business. The house had become too small for the four children and the in-laws. The in-laws moved to an apartment that had just become vacant in the house of the Stern family. This apartment was rather acceptable. A few weeks later, on a Friday, both parents had a stroke on the same day. Father recovered from this illness within a short time, but Mother never fully recovered. Her mental capacity was diminished even when her physical strength slowly recovered.

At that time, I observed with fear the way our youngest child was developing. All the small signs of development that give one pleasure, as one observes a developing child, were missing. In spite of good nutrition and expectations, nothing was happening with the child, which caused us serious concerns for her. At the age of nine months she became ill. Dr. Bendowski, who took over as the district's physician from Dr. Cohn, treated the child with great care but had no success. We also enlisted the help of the new physician, Dr. Rubensohn, but he too was not successful. She died at 10 p.m. on August 10. Dr. Rubensohn was of the opinion that the child would never have developed into a normal child. This was again a bitter chalice that fate had given us.

The fact that my parents were now living near by in Posen meant that I could now see them more frequently. None the less, Mother rushed to us as soon as she heard the news. My mother, who previously was so active in the business, could now devote all her time to the running of the household. As a result of this, my sister Jettchen was left with little to do around the home. My parents were glad to send her to help me. She herself was glad to come, for weeks on end, to us in Graetz.

Although my father-in-law was not able to do much in his last years and my mother-in-law was no longer of any help in the business, both were able to keep an eye on outsiders, who were helping in the business.

After they retired from the business, I became more and more involved in it, especially as my husband was often away on business trips. The assistance of my sister in running the household was even more needed and appreciated, especially as one only had the minimal amount of help, and the little children needed supervision.

At this time the brick factory in Gradowice was blooming even more, and a new plant in Rostarschewo was being erected. Moreover, my husband was busy with two forestry businesses in Kunowo and Sarbia, which required his frequent absences from our town. Together with Mr. M. D. Cohn, he established a factory that produced roof coverings [*likely tiles*]. His creative spirit did not rest, and he constantly expanded his area of activities.

As a result of this, I became more and more responsible for the local part of the business. It was not easy, but it granted me great satisfaction to be able to help in growing the business. Based on today's circumstances, the conditions under which we had begun our business were very moderate. The fact that for nine years we kept house with the parents meant that we had smaller needs for both parts of the family. Moreover, at that time one lived under very modest conditions and did not enjoy any luxuries, which allowed us to make real financial progress during these nine years.

I forgot to mention that toward the end of the year 1869, an Advancement Organization was formed in Graetz, under the urging of my husband. He was then elected as its director and led the organization in the formation of a local Discount Bank. In his great loyalty, my husband was there daily during working hours. The flourishing of this institute can be attributed, to a large extent, to his dedication. In the year 1870, the trust of his fellow citizens caused him to be elected to the town council. Our children, for whom these memories are written, know what he had accomplished in that role and later as chairman of the town council.

At the same time, my husband was also elected to the Board of the Jewish Community, and, in spite of the fact that the Board included many older people, the Board elected him to its chair. A few years later, at the urging of his friends, and against my wishes, he accepted the role as first chairman of the community. He held this position until we left for Berlin.

With the passage of time he was accorded more and more honorable positions. The town asked him to serve as its representative in the local district's board. The Organization of the German Metal Traders, which was based in Berlin and which he had helped to establish, elected him to be its chairman. I was rather flabbergasted when I heard this news. Many very important owners of businesses that were located in Berlin, Dresden, Hanover, Emden, etc., belonged to the board of this organization.

Nonetheless, they selected as their chairman the small businessman from the small town of Graetz. This gave my husband considerable happiness and made me very proud of him. Of course, all these honors brought with them also many additional burdens. When one realizes that at the same time our own growing business required a lot of time, it is obvious that this also resulted in much additional activity for his "Partner," as he always called me.

I performed all these duties gladly and happily, as his praises were my highest rewards. Fortunately, the business was strictly closed on Saturdays, which assured us of one quiet day per week. As Sunday was the busiest day of the week, this assured us that at least we had time to be with the children and could also do something for our own general education. On nice days, we also took the children for a hike in the afternoon. The fact that during the working days we could not spend enough time with the children meant that we could not just hire any old children's maid. We had to look for an educated maid instead.

In response to an advertisement, several candidates showed up. Among those who had responded was a Miss Kaul, who came from Posen. She became the guardian of our little ones for the next six years. Salomon was two-and-one-half years old when she arrived.

On Saturday, June 22, 1878, while the other three children were taking a walk with Miss Kaul, our Hedwig [*future wife of Julius Brodnitz*] was born. A couple of days prior to this, my mother had come to stay with us in order to take care of me and to help me during that time. The child prospered in the care of a good wet nurse. I also recovered faster than in the past.

In the fall of that year [1878], we celebrated the seventieth birthday of my father and the engagement of my sister Jettchen [*Eugenie, also called Jenny*]. This allowed all the children of the Badt family to get together again. In January of 1879, the golden anniversary of my in-laws was celebrated. My sister Jettchen married Simon Krombach February 6, 1879. That year during the month of May, which was in that year especially cold, I became ill with rheumatic fever, which caused me to become incapacitated for a long while. The fingers of both hands became swollen, and the joints were seriously infected. My husband was in Berlin when this started, and I had to stay in bed and could not move my fingers. My fingers were covered with cotton bandages so that my food had to be cut for me.

My sister-in-law Roeschen was stricken at the same time by a similar affliction in her left arm. Both our husbands insisted that these problems had to be addressed in the most extreme manner. We therefore went to Wiesbaden at the beginning of July. In the meantime, the pain had subsided so that we could travel joyfully. In Wiesbaden, we took a daily bath. By about noon, we were always done with the treatment, and in the afternoon, we took beautiful hikes in the surrounding area. During the last week, we went on a steamboat for a tour on the river Rhein from Bieberich to Koblenz. One afternoon, we also went by train to Ems and returned by train to Wiesbaden in the same evening. We considered ourselves extremely lucky to have had this opportunity. We were granted the opportunity to visit the storied shores of the river Rhein, which were most enjoyable to see. In those days traveling was not very common.

Upon returning home to Graetz, the place, at first, did not appeal to us at all. We missed especially the wonderful hikes. Instead, we had the pleasure of being with our husbands and children and in our own home. We would not have liked to live in Wiesbaden without them.

In January 1880, our youngest child was suddenly hit by an infection. Dr. Rubensohn, who was now our family physician and who proved to be very capable, prescribed her medications. After one week, she had recovered. My husband checked with the doctor, who assured him that all was well. Thereupon, he traveled to the wedding of a cousin in Nakel. On the following day, the child was suddenly suffering from a renewed infection and almost choked to death. The doctor declared that he would have to operate on the child but that he would need the help of a colleague. Dr. Bendowski was called, and he rushed to our place. I held the child while the preparations were underway, and she became blue in the face, as she had more and more difficulties in breathing. When they were ready to take the child from me, she suddenly developed a strong cough, which took care of the crisis at hand and negated the need for an urgent surgery. It took a long while before the child was fully recovered. Because she had a residual hoarseness, it was necessary to prevent the child from crying, as the doctor was concerned that such crying could cause a reinfection. This required that we let the child get away with everything, which she discovered very soon and put to good use.

On March 13, another little girl appeared whom we named Betty. It is not known why, whether because of the excitement of the past few months or because of some other reasons, in spite of careful care and changing of wet nurses, the child just did not develop properly. She died on July 4, 1880, at the age of four months, of an enlarged spleen.

I was seriously run down and also suffered from awful migraine headaches and, therefore, the doctor decided that I must get away. As, according to the doctor, Rosa was disposed to depression, we were supposed to go together to Colberg. We left at the end of July. Although our stay was only three weeks long, it did both of us a lot of good.

Our Hugo saw the light of day on April 2, 1881. On the Saturday before Passover he was circumcised, in the presence of my parents, sisters Krombach, and my sister Jettchen. This time all went smoothly, and a good wet nurse cared for the child. Within a short time, he blossomed like a red apple.

During the next summer, we planned to expand the back end of our house onto property that we had purchased from old Mr.

Neumann. This property had a wide expense of land in the back. Our own rooms had already become too small for the business. For the added line of oven tiles, we needed additional space, and so we located these products in what was later to become the Zweigers Hotel. We also needed more space for the increased line of rod irons. The construction began and proceeded in a rapid clip.

On the occasion of a trip to Berlin, I urged my husband to consult a specialist, as he had a growth on the top of his right cheek, right under his temple. This raised area did not respond to the various creams. The local doctor said that he could remove this growth by an operation. My husband then went to Professor Bardeleben, who suggested that he stay in his clinic for eight days of treatment. As Father was not prepared for an extended stay, he returned home. He next got in touch with Dr. Pauly in Posen, who had a good reputation as a surgeon. He made up his mind to have Dr. Pauly carry out what was supposed to be a minor operation. The outcome was rather different. We don't know whether it happened because of an accident or if it could have been avoided. Our local doctor would not express an opinion. In any case, while the growth was removed, the saliva gland and a nerve that controls the facial muscles were also cut, resulting in the paralysis of these facial muscles. The man who was full of energy and strong will power and body came back home after eight days in a shape that brought me close to despair. Whereas before the operation, Father would be the first one in the household to be up in the morning, driving the children and the staff to get going, he could now only be active for a short time, before he retired apologizing, "I can't go on." You can well imagine how I felt guilt because I did not stand up in a more insistent manner that the operation should be carried out in Berlin, where this paralysis might not have occurred.

I had to make sure that Father did not notice my despair. Often after he had fallen asleep, I cried into my pillow. During the day, however, activities were so pressing that they filled my day with duties. Dr. Rubensohn stood by our side and, with much understanding, took care of the rehabilitation. As soon as Father was able to travel, he sent him to a nerves specialist, Dr. Berger in Breslau, where he stayed for a few days. From this doctor he learned how to massage the facial muscles and how to treat the area with cold water. He also gave him a suitable treatment with electricity.

Upon returning home, Father went to Dr. Rubensohn for electric treatment. In July, Father went on a rehabilitation trip to Kissingen, as he had lost much weight. In Kissingen and, after that, at home, the treatment continued. With the passage of time the condition slowly improved. After one year the deformed face and the drooping eyelid were almost back to their former form. Only the twitching of the affected muscles remained. This also stopped after a time.

To my joy, my husband's improved physical condition was also accompanied by the return of his former ability to be active in all else. Only the scar remained in future years as a reminder of this bad period. This period forced me to become more independent and understanding of the activities of the business. This caused Father to give me more responsibly for running the business. He only intervened when I asked for his advice. All this excitement did not happen without leaving its impact on me. I frequently suffered from intensive pain, which the doctor attributed to gall stones. In the summer of 1882, I had to go for a *Kur* [*medical spa*] to Karlsbad. I traveled there with my sister-in-law Roeschen, who was also prescribed a *Kur* visit.

For those of us who lived in a small-town environment, Karlsbad and its international life offered a most exciting and interesting place. We used the beautiful surroundings of Karlsbad to go for trips and hikes. We also had the opportunity to meet nice and interesting people so that the *Kur* offered not only a time for refreshing the body but also a period of mental awakening. As a result of this stay, the following winter also passed well.

Miss Kaul left us on April 1, 1883. She could no longer handle Ernst, who was by now eight years old. Our dear Rosa left at about the same time to attend school in Posen. She had by then completed all the grades available in the school in Graetz. She was living at the pension of Mrs. Mueldauer, which was, at the time, the only Jewish boarding house in Posen. At first I thought that I could manage without help. I realized very quickly that I needed a better supervisor for the children. In response to an advertisement, a Miss Behrend from Marienburg showed up. She reported to work at the end of June. She had just enough time to settle down in our home when, on July 8, 1883, our dear Bianka arrived.

In the previous periods, my mother had always come to help before the birth of our children. This time she could not come, as she had been taking care of her sick husband. On August 18 [*1883*], when Bianka was six weeks old, my dear father passed away. His loss had a deep impact on me. My siblings and I stayed with Mother for the seven days of mourning. Shortly after that, Mother celebrated her seventieth birthday.

Let me add here, that on March 1, 1882, my mother-in-law died after a prolonged sickness. As nurses were not available in Graetz in those days, we took turns in taking care of her at night, with the relatives of the Stern family.

Bianka had a good wet nurse and developed nicely. While I was bedridden, we had a maid who took care of running the household. After three weeks, I took over my regular duties. When she first came, Miss Behrend knew very little about running a household. She quickly learned how to do it, and our children also had a good relationship with her. Rosa came home for her school vacation, while Father went again to Kissingen, which was good for his stomach.

The health problems, which I had mentioned before, reoccurred in the course of the following winter. The doctor recommended that I should go to Karlsbad as soon as possible. I left at the end of

May and met there with my friends, the Brombergs, with whom I had struck a close friendship two years earlier. This friendship was now renewed. We used the period to go on hikes, and we had a good time together. At this *Kur*, I stayed only three weeks.

While I was away, my husband demolished the house next door that we had purchased from the Neumanns. On the ground floor he built instead a dining room and a laundry and, above it, two rooms for the children, which we urgently needed for our growing family. When the construction was nearly complete, we went together to Posen one afternoon and ordered the furniture for the new dining room. This was completed within three hours as was the selection of new carpeting. After a short visit to mother's place, we returned home.

The new furniture arrived on the day before New Year's, and the room was already prepared to receive it. With the New Year we expanded into the very pretty new room, from which we derived many years of pleasure.

On this occasion, the *Kur* at Karlsbad had only limited lasting effect. When the winter came, I began to suffer from frequent attacks of pain, which I was able to overcome (and avoided becoming bedridden) only by concentrating all my willpower on it. I needed to take the treatments at Karlsbad during the next three years to reduce the pain. Only then did I finally get rid of them.

The next few years passed without any special events. One carried out one's duty and lived with the family. Only the frequent trips, which dear Father had to take for the business or in connection with his official functions, brought about occasionally new stimulations.

The children kept growing and one had both the pleasure as well as the concerns about them. For a short time, Lenchen and Ernst attended the local elementary school. When Ernst was eight years old, he switched to a Boys School, which was founded in Graetz at Father's initiative. When he got transferred to that school, Ernst was promoted to the fifth grade. Not long after that a Sisters School [*a girl's school*] was formed in our town. Lenchen was enrolled into the second grade while Hedwig started her studies there in the lowest grade. The children were all rather capable, and the girls did their assigned work under the supervision of Miss Behrend. Ernst, on the other hand, was not inclined to do his schoolwork. He was therefore left under my direct control.

Rosa, who studied with eagerness and success at the Luise School in Posen, was suffering from low blood levels. Although we did not want to disrupt her studies, we thought that the conditions at the house of Mrs. Mueldauer, where she was residing, left much to be desired. We therefore took her back home at Easter time in 1886, in spite of her and our wish that she stay and complete her studies in Posen. Rosa stayed with us at home during that summer. On October 1, we took her to Berlin, where she stayed with Mrs. Silbermann to study foreign languages and music. She was also expected to become a bit more skillful and self-sufficient.

I found Mrs. Silbermann to be a very pleasant person to whom I could entrust my children.

Rosa was also very happy there, and when the time came for her to leave the house of Mrs. Silbermann on July 1, 1887, she was rather reluctant to do so. Upon Rosa's return to our home, Miss Behrend left us in order to move to Berlin and search for a new working environment. Lenchen, with her active temper, did not have a good relationship with Miss Behrend. As a result, I was frequently summoned upstairs to arbitrate between these two.

My father-in-law died on July 12, 1887, after being bedridden for several weeks. Sisters Stern had sold their business a short while before this event and had gone together on a *Kur* trip to Wiesbaden. Helene Breslauer was sent by her parents to Graetz after the death of the grandmother in order to make sure that the grandfather would not be there all alone. But she could not be expected to take care of him alone. Therefore, sister-in-law Nettchen came for a few weeks and we all shared the responsibility. At the end of the seven days of mourning, my doctor insisted that I needed to relax. He suggested that I travel to Warmbrunn in order also to get care for my hands, which were subject to rheumatism, so that they would be ready for the coming winter.

I went on this trip with Rosa, while my mother came to Graetz to take up my responsibilities in the house. Although the warm baths were not much of a success in treating the rheumatism, in general the stay was of great help, and Rosa and I returned home in much better shape, ready to tackle our regular tasks with renewed vigor.

Hugo also started attending school in April 1887. Pastor Haedrich established a school for young boys, which sounded promising but turned out to be less than a success. Other parents of children who attended this school were dissatisfied. We all requested the town administration to admit young boys into the lower grades of the Sisters School. Hugo attended this school until the fifth grade. When he reached the fifth grade, he transferred to the Boys School. He also had difficulties in concentrating on his homework. Ernst was confirmed [Bar Mitzvah] in March of 1887. As the Boys School did not have the upper grades, we had to send him to the high school in Posen in April 1888. The residence of Mrs. Dr. Hirschfeld was recommended to us. Her son, who had studied languages, supervised the fellows. A few months later, after Ernst was already in the house, Dr. Hirschfeld was appointed to a position at the Montefiore Foundation in Ramsgate. Her daughter, who was a trained teacher, took over the running of the boarding house. This was not the right place for Ernst. A family by the name of Wiener, who had a son of similar age who was a good student and was supposed to be a good example for Ernst, took him in. The result was less then satisfactory, and only with the help of private lessons did he manage to get into the upper grades of the high school.

In June of 1889, Hugo Brodnitz asked for the hand of our dear Rosa in marriage. The young couple met through our nephew Isidor Stern. On the occasion of a visit of a few days in Posen, during which time we had also met with the distinguished Brodnitz parents, Rosa and Hugo expressed their wish to be married. Rosa, with our full consent, got engaged at that time, although the occasion was not publicized at once. This was the case as only a few days earlier Regina Jablonski, the daughter of our sister Stern, who was very dear to us, had died in Magdeburg. From all that we learned about the intended groom of Rosa and the Brodnitz family, we felt that we could leave the fate of our eldest child with our future son-in-law without any qualms. We felt this way, even though it was not easy for us, and especially for me, to get used to the idea that we were parting when our child was still so young [*she was 18 years old*].

Julie Badt Herzfeld, likely in the 1880s or 1890s

The period that was left until the actual wedding was, naturally, rather hectic. To purchase the trousseau required numerous trips to Posen. These resulted in stays of several days and got us often together with Hugo's parents. These meetings also brought us ever nearer to our future *mechuttonim* [*in-laws*]. The friendliness, charm, and full-of-goodwill ways of Papa Brodnitz were very much appreciated, as was the dramatic sense of humor of Mama Brodnitz, which was rather amusing. During the visits to their nice and comfortable home, I always felt closely attached to them. Most of the time, after our shopping days, Rosa and I spent the evening with the Brodnitz family.

During the following summer, the doctor considered it desirable for me to go on a *Kur* trip to Salzbrunn. I used the period of low activity, during the school vacation, for this purpose. That had a disadvantage for Rosa, as she had to supervise not only the children of our own family but also Lenchen Badt, one of the Mielziners, as well as another child who came to spend the summer in our house. It would have been difficult enough for Rosa to keep all of them in check. On top of that, she had to supervise the help in the house. In a small village such as ours, it was difficult to get good help. During that time in particular, we had a less than efficient maid working for us. As a result, Rosa had to take part in all that went on in the house. When her fiancé was coming to visit on a Sunday afternoon, Rosa was kept busy supervising the kitchen until eleven a.m., and then she had to change in a great hurry and get ready to fetch Hugo at the train station at noon.

During the fall of that year Father was busy subdividing the property that was between Paulshof and Wielichowo, which took him away from home for extended periods of time but which turned out to be rather profitable. In October, he also had to spend two weeks in Messeritz in a meeting of business owners. However, thanks to goodwill on everyone's part, everything worked out well.

On December 17, 1889, the wedding [*of Rosa and Hugo*] took place in Posen. As these were the eldest children from both families, all felt that they had to take part in this feast, including all the children. A total of ninety-four people took part in that occasion. A few days later, the young couple traveled to Dresden and they came back in time for the New Year. At that time, Germany was attacked for the first time by the influenza bug. When I traveled to Posen on New Year's Eve to welcome back the young couple,

Hugo's mother was already suffering from the first case of the disease. As I was unaware that this was a sickness that is easily passed by exposure, I did not try to keep my distance from Mama Brodnitz. On my trip back home from Posen, I was shaking from the sickness but I was fearful of getting stuck on the way, until I made it home. After that all the members of our household came down with the influenza. Father was the last one to get sick but his illness lasted the longest. Fortunately, the young couple had stayed in Posen and was not affected by the infection.

In the past, we had traveled to Posen only rarely. Now that the children were living in Posen, we used all possible opportunities to travel there [*Graetz is 46 km west-southwest of Posen*]. The children also came frequently for Sunday visits to us so that we were able to stay in regular touch.

Even before Rosa got engaged, Lenchen was residing in a boarding house in Berlin. She attended the upper grade of the Doerstlig School. In addition, as was customary with Mrs. Silbermann, where Lenchen resided, she took private music and art history lessons. Two months before Rosa's wedding, she came back home in order to take over the care of her younger siblings and the household from Rosa.

Ernst befriended Hugo's brother Hermann [*Brodnitz*]. They were of similar age and attended the same grade at the high school. They became fast friends, a friendship that has lasted through the years. Perhaps as the result of Hermann's good example, Ernst became a better student from that time on.

In February of 1891, we decided to tear down the old home that we had inherited from the parents and replace it with a new building. For many years prior, we had the intention to do this. However, as we sold out all the brick tiles [*these were produced in their factory for sale in their store*] each winter, none were left for us. We also were concerned about the difficulties that such a move entailed, as our business and home were one and the same.

As might have been expected, the building period entailed a lot of work. Just relocating the display rooms to our other building across the way was a difficult task. Separating the display rooms from the warehouse (which stayed in its old location) also caused some difficulties.

In September, we were ready to move the business back to the old location. As the display rooms were bigger and nicer and the entrance to the basement was nearby, it was much easier to show our products and to serve the customers.

The new building also provided us with nicer living quarters, which we then started to refurbish with nicer furniture.

I went to Karlsbad in June of 1892. On the way back, I stopped over in Berlin, where I bought furniture for the new hall and bedrooms. On the occasion of our silver anniversary, on October 30, 1892, the new rooms were consecrated. Many friends and relatives joined us for the festive occasion, which was both nice and harmonious.

The local municipal authorities, the discount bank, and the leaders of the Jewish community all provided numerous awards and honors to recognize Father's many contributions to the social well-being of the community.

In Easter of 1893, we brought our Hugo to Posen to study at the high school. At the suggestion of my mother, he was left in the care of the teacher, Jakobsohn. This teacher lived in the same house as my mother and sister Krombach.

He did rather well in the first year at the high school and was promoted to the next grade, at the end of the school year.

Our daughter Lenchen [*Helene*] got engaged [*to Samuel Meyer*] in May of 1893. During the frequent visits by the intended groom we had learned to appreciate the good qualities of our future second son-in-law. We had not met the mother and siblings of this person. We only met them at the time of the actual wedding. His mother proved to be a very nice and pleasant lady with much dignity. In the following years we often met them while we were visiting Stargard as well as when we visited their home in Noerenberg. This led to mutual closeness that added to the pleasure of getting closer together.

The wedding [*of Lenchen and Samuel Meyer*] was celebrated in Graetz on August 22, 1893. This was a very nice celebration except for the fact that the weather was extremely hot on that day. Fewer people were present at the wedding than at Rosa's wedding, but our very dear and near relatives were all there. Even my dear mother came. On the day before the wedding she had become a great-grandmother, when Walter, the eldest son of Lenchen Katschke, was born [*this Lenchen, or Helene, was the daughter of Julie's brother Louis Badt*].

The young couple went on an extended honeymoon, as their place in Stargard was only ready by October 1.

Rosa came for an extended visit in September, as Hugo went on a trip to the resort at Baden-Baden. She stayed until after the Jewish New Year and helped pack Lenchen's wedding gifts and trousseau, which were all sent initially to us in Graetz.

Hedwig was sent to Berlin on October 1, 1893, upon graduating from the Sisters School in Graetz. She was also sent to live with Mrs. Silbermann, who proved to be so effective when she had our two older daughters.

At Rosa's recommendation, we hired Miss Flatau to help me in running the house and to enable me to take a day or two off. We visited with the newly married couple in Stargard over Christmas of 1893. They seemed very happy in their new apartment.

On February 24 of 1894, we were surprised when our oldest son [*Ernst*] passed with success the high school graduation examination. We had expected that at the earliest, he would only graduate at the month of March.

The confirmation [*Bar Mitzvah*] of Hugo took place in April of 1894. All our dear children came to join us on that occasion.

Lenchen informed us that we could expect to become grandparents later that year, news that brought us much joy.

Our first grandson [*Kurt Meyer*] was born on September 4, 1894. Father was at that time on a business trip to Berlin. I dropped everything in the house and rushed on the next train to Stargard [*Stargard Szczecinski, 37 km east-southeast of Stettin (Szcein)*] to help in taking care of Lenchen. On arriving in Stargard, I found there a solid boy, and all was proceeding as it should. The *brit* could, therefore, take place eight days after the birth. Father traveled directly to Stargard where, with our closest family, we celebrated the event.

To our sadness, Hugo could not come from Posen. Hugo's mother, with whom I had gone to Karlsbad only a few short months ago, was hit by a serious illness from which she died in December of that year [*1894*]. This was a terrible painful blow for us, as a very close and friendly relationship had developed between these relatives and us. The funeral took place on Christmas Day, and we attended the service.

Long before these events, I had told my siblings in Glogau that I was going to visit them. This was the first chance for me to go to visit them since they had moved to there from Sorau. I did not want to cancel this visit and, therefore, went to them right after the funeral. I stayed with them until the third day of Christmas. I was very glad to see that my sister-in-law Regina [*Regina Badt who married Isidor Badt, Julie's brother*] kept a well-organized household. In the past we did not think much of her capabilities as a homemaker. Now, we found that she was running a well-maintained home and was able to draw on the help of their eldest daughter, Martha. As my brother was also doing well, I had real pleasure from this visit.

Ernst went to Freiburg, with his friend Hermann Brodnitz, to take up the first semester of his law studies at the local university. For the second and third semester, both transferred to Munich, where my nephew Alfred Badt [*the eldest son of Isidor and Regina Badt*] was studying medicine. A rather unpleasant surprise awaited me when Ernst came on his first visit from Munich. A sword had left its marks on Ernst's smooth face. It took a long time before I got over seeing my young son disfigured in such a way. I could never understand why one would flaunt such a disfigurement [*we don't know the story behind this mark but assume it was from a duel*].

In 1895 he transferred to Berlin, where he rented an apartment together with Alfred [*Badt*]. We, as parents found this arrangement to be rather good as we thought that Alfred, who was much sounder in his studies, would be a positive influence on Ernst, who was more flighty. As I found out when I visited Berlin, on the occasion of the Bar Mitzvah of my nephew Leo Mielziner [*1896*], Ernst also had a very positive influence on Alfred, who was a square and socially rather helpless.

By now, our Hugo reached his adolescent years and did not want to put in any effort at school. In the residence where he was staying, he was also involved in some friction so that we felt that it was necessary to change his environment. In response to an advertisement that we placed, we received many replies. Over the course of two days, we checked out the various responders and selected the home of the Zillinski family. They showed a keen interest in the boy and they also developed mutually good relations. This can best be seen by the fact that he maintained close contact with this family during and after his days as a student. When he was injured falling off his bike, while doing his work-study at the Urbanowski Factory, the Zillinski family cared for him as if he were one of them.

In Easter 1897, when Hugo was given his middle school certificate and was promoted to the eleventh grade, he said that he wanted to leave school at the following Easter. The likelihood of his getting any further promotion at school appeared dim, so we considered it useless to force him to stay at the high school. As

Hugo wanted to become an electric technician, he had to gain a year of practical experience before he could attend a higher technical school. He, therefore, went to work as a trainee at the Urbanowski Factory.

In the meantime, Ernst went to Breslau for his last two semesters of studies. After a year's stay with Mrs. Silbermann, Hedwig returned home and, like her elder sisters before her, she started to help in running the household. From time to time she traveled to visit her married sisters, and on one occasion we went together to recover our strength at a resort in Misdroy.

During the summer of 1896, our honorable in-law Samuel Brodnitz died after a lengthy sickness. My dear husband was in Landeck for a *Kur* and was, therefore, unable to attend the funeral. In June of 1897, Ernst and his friend Hermann [*Brodnitz*] passed the examination for trainees in civil service. It caused us special pleasure to learn that they passed the test, in spite of the fact that they had to take the oral test in front of the so-called "Death Committee of Examiners."

As my lungs required some fresh air, I had to travel to Reichenhall. Ernst came along to get some rest. During the prior year, our family doctor sent me for a *Kur* to Pyrmont, to which I had gone with Aunt Nettchen. In Pyrmont I was under the care of an understanding doctor who paid much attention, and I gained some weight as my body was severely undernourished. The doctor in Pyrmont prescribed that I eat rye soup in the morning on an empty stomach, which resulted in my gaining weight, which took me from 102 pounds to 120 pounds during the course of the winter.

The stay at the resort in Reichenhall was meant to confirm this gain.

Ernst and I traveled at first to Berlin. In the evening we went from there by a special train via Munich to Reichenhall. We would have liked to stop over in Munich, but that could not be done. We arrived in Reichenhall rather tired at four o'clock. We were met by Mrs. Jeanette Salomon from Posen, with whose help we soon located a suitable apartment. Each morning after breakfast, we left for a walk, from which we came back at lunchtime. In the meantime I followed the ordered *Kur,* and in the afternoon we went together on additional walks. In this way, we were able to carry out all the worthwhile hikes. We also went on some full-day excursions to places such as Berchtesgaden, Koenigssee, and Salzburg. I was completely enchanted by the natural beauty that that area had offered in such abundance. The crowning piece of the visit was the trip to Berchtesgaden-Koenigssee. We traveled there in the company of very pleasant and jolly people who talked us into visiting a local mine.

After fourteen days, we received a telegram from home saying that Ernst was hired for a position in Lobses and had to return home as soon as possible. At the same time, the continual nice weather that we had until then also came to an end. The rest of my stay was so drenched by the repeated rain that I decided to cut short my stay. This turned out to be very lucky, as my train was the last one to make it to Munich before the tracks were flooded. After my train passed, all traffic on that route was stopped for a whole week.

I stayed in Munich for two days where I saw how much that city had to offer. I then traveled home via Berlin. On the return trip I saw the awful devastation that was brought about by two weeks of heavy rain. The floods that I saw were most severe in the area of Wittenberg, where all one could see were dirty flooded fields.

On returning home I entered eagerly into the normal routine work, as there was much to do.

In all these reports, I must now come back to some of the events that took place in the business during the years 1888 to 1897. Father's active spirit, which always led him to search for new opportunities, led him to take part in a major project that, had it succeeded, would have made him in one move into a very rich man. Induced by a search for coal on the property of the brick factory, he got in touch with a recommended specialist by the name of Friedrich Guetler. The test drillings ended without positive results. Guetler, who was an optimist by nature, told Father in confidence that in Posen there were good chances for discovering coal in the ground. He got Father interested in carrying out test drilling. They drilled in secret on the property of Johannismuehle, under close monitoring. Once the owners of the property figured out the true purpose of the drilling, they had to be taken as partners. The drilling reached brown coal at a depth of eighty meters.

Father requested at once the mineral rights for the property from the appropriate mining board, which resided at that time in the town of Goerlitz. A Mr. von Rosenberg then accompanied Father to Posen, and once the presence of coal was confirmed, mining rights were granted for the area in question. Once the mining permit was issued, the plans to mine the coal become publicly known in the city and district of Posen. This caused many to envy our good luck.

In order to secure the wider surrounding area around Posen, further test drilling took place in great haste and the mineral rights for seven additional fields were secured. Father had the idea that he would be content with the mineral rights. He thought that it would require more funds to unseal these treasures than he and his partners, who owned half of the partnership, had at their disposal. His idea was to transfer his rights to a more potent organization, in return for a share of the enterprise. The mining official, Mr. von Rosenberg, was able to exert his influence on one of the partners, with whom he stayed frequently during his visits to Posen, to get the partnership to start at once with the digging of a pit. As a professional expert, he calculated that the first pit could be dug for 20,000 Deutschmarks. To preserve the peace, Father went along with his partner's wish.

The digging of the pit began, and soon thereafter excitement began to enter our life. At a time when there was pressing work at home, telegrams started to arrive. They required Father's urgent presence at the site, because the four other partners, who were located near the site, could not resolve some issue. The year of 1888, with its heavy rains, caused us much harm. On top of that, with the technical skills at the time, one could not effectively fight the water that penetrated into the pit. All the methods that were available at that time were tried, including some of the largest pumps, mixing in cement and building it up with concrete. With every step that one took forward, new problems were uncovered. At the end, after about 80,000 Deutschmarks were swallowed up by the project, one no longer had the courage to go forward with the enterprise. At this point the partners regretted that they had not followed Father's suggestion.

Soon after the project had begun, the cigarette factory Venzke became a partner and held 25 percent of the venture. From the 37 percent that Father held, he parted with 5 percent, by assigning them to Uncle Krombach, who wished to participate in this luck. As a result of this, Father's part in the enterprise was lowered to 32.5 percent [*this share was cited in the original document*]. Although this reduced the risk, our loss from this venture was 20,000 Deutschmarks. This was subtracted, starting in 1888, from the year-end balance, until only 200 Deutschmarks were left on the books. Multiple attempts to finance the enterprise always resulted in failure. With that, the so-called "luck," that caused everyone to be jealous of us, came to an end.

At the same time in 1888, while we were in the thick of the fray and all its excitement, there was also an issue regarding the financing of a brewery in Graetz. An English firm planned the construction, in which Father and M. Werner of Posen and some gentlemen from Breslau were to participate. After much effort and many trips to Berlin and Posen, etc., this project also collapsed, which led to a major lawsuit. This case was led by Werner and resulted, after years of litigation, in poor returns. Father was supposed to be the commercial manager, and Baehnisch was going to be the technical director of the projected incorporated company. The English people lost the 100,000 Deutschmarks, which they had paid on account. Of this amount, the local brewer in Graetz got 40,000 Deutschmarks, which Father received. From this he paid himself and the other agents of the company. Baehnisch swallowed 60,000 Deutschmarks, which he did not want to share with the others. This led to another lawsuit.

Also in 1888, Father purchased, together with a certain Mr. Salinger, a property called Zabikowo Manner, which was located in Stenschewo near Posen. Father conditioned his participation in this transaction on Mr. Salinger agreeing to give Uncle Krombach a one-third part in the deal. Mr. Salinger took possession of the property and leased the brick factory that was located on the property. All would have been discharged swiftly had the leaser of the brick factory not gotten into financial difficulties. While Father was away in Koblenz for a meeting of the brick manufacturers' organization, he took a pleasure trip to Holland. In Amsterdam, he received an urgent telegram, asking him to go at once to Posen to settle the problems. The lease was revoked, and Uncle Krombach and Father took over the running of the factory.

As Uncle had no prior experience with brick production, Father gave him the training in the business and, in return for minimal compensation, he became the sole owner of the factory. This provided Uncle with a better income than his previous business, which involved trading in Posen. As the construction of fortifications in the area of Posen created a significant demand for bricks, the brick producers in the area prospered and, before too long, Uncle could give up his trading business. This allowed our aunt to have a much more pleasant life. Father was always glad to see that the project progressed so well. When Uncle was lost to the family at an early age, Father was especially glad that the aunt and her children were left well provided for.

After this business was resolved, brick factories were built with Schwesens in Hohensalza and with Uncle Breslauer from Schrimm. Later on, together with Mr. Moses from Bromberg, they established the Brick Plant Brahnau in Bromberg. Whereas the first factory was successful from the start, the second plant had many problems. Some of the issues had to do with the raw material that was used. Other problems originated from defective equipment. In any case, these issues required a lot of Father's time and energy. At long last, Father agreed with Uncle Breslauer to separate from the participation in this factory and leave it to Uncle. Our own brick factories in Gradowice and Rothenburg, which Father had run and supervised alone, had prospered under his care.

With all these business events, the year 1898 arrived. Shortly after the Jewish Pesach, my mother became ill at the age of 84. She was ill for 14 days, in the course of which I traveled frequently to see her in Posen. On May 9, 1898, she was taken from her children and grandchildren. I spent the first days of mourning in Posen with my four siblings. During that time I noticed already that Uncle Krombach was belching and had stomach trouble.
As it turned out he was suffering from an incurable sickness. He, however, believed Professor Leuber, who told him that he would get better on his own.

In April of 1898, we sold our construction materials business. The location was leased and taken over by Arthur Loewinshon. Based on the advice of Professor Gerhard from Berlin, whom I saw in the fall of 1897, I was supposed to quit my daily activities in the business because of my continued coughing. Father stated that without my help, he could not continue running the business.

So, after careful consideration, it was decided to sell the business. The sale took place in April of 1898, and it required a lot of effort on my part. After that, however, life became much easier for me, as I only had to supervise the household, with the help of our daughter. I also helped a bit in running the brick factories.

Shortly before the first of April 1898, contracts were signed for the reorganization of the brick factories. The three factories in Gradowice and the three in Rothenburg had achieved economic self-sufficiency. Mr. Krause took over the factories located in Rothenburg, while Father took over the ones in Gradowice. Father hired a Mr. Jaeger, who had worked for us in the warehouse, to run the plants. I helped train this man.

These changes allowed us for once to be away from our home at the same time. We used this advantage to travel to Stargard over Pentecost. Our daughters Hedwig and Bianka were invited during this time to visit with Rosa in Posen. This visit had an important impact on the future of our dear Hedwig. Hugo's brother Julius [*Julius Brodnitz*] was also visiting Posen at that time. While they were together, the affection that both already had for each other increased to the point that Julius asked for Hedwig's hand in marriage. In the following week, Father celebrated his sixtieth birthday. All the children and both sons-in-law gathered on that day in our home to celebrate the day. Hugo and Rosa gave us an indication of Julius' intentions, and we, as parents, gave our happy consent. A few days later, Rosa came again to visit us. She came at the request of Julius, in order to obtain Hedwig's consent. Hedwig agreed gladly, and a few days after that, the engagement took place.

These were the first happy days since the death of my mother. It was decided that Hedwig and I would go for relaxation to Landeck and Julius was to join us there. As I was busy packing and getting the house ready for the trip, I developed some bleeding. Our family doctor was very helpful in getting me well again. He insisted, however, that I go to Reichenhall and not to Landeck.

Bianka, for whom brine baths were ordered, went to Hohensalza, while at the beginning of July, I traveled with Hedwig to Reichenhall. When the courts began their vacation, in the middle of July, Julius followed us to that resort. We spent some very enjoyable days together, which were dampened only by the excessive heat. As I still had to be careful, Father took the young couple on some of the nice outings while I stayed back with friends. On the return trip, I spent a day in Posen to order the dowry. Once Julius located an apartment and had it readied, the wedding day was set for October 30, which was also our wedding day. Hedwig was welcomed with open arms as a member of the family by Julius' siblings. All were deeply sorrowed by the fact that the elder Brodnitzes had not lived to be present for this occasion [*Samuel Brodnitz had died June 19, 1896, and his wife, Rosalie, had died on December 21, 1894*]. The families of the bride and groom, as well as many friends and relatives, took part in the ceremony. The death of Uncle Krombach four weeks before the wedding day cast a shadow on the event, although this ending relieved him of his ongoing pain and suffering.

During Christmas of 1898, we went for an eight-day-long visit to our children in Berlin. We were glad to see our children's luck and happiness and we returned home feeling that all was very satisfactory.

I was supposed to go to Reichenhall again during the summer. As Father did not want to stay there for a long visit, I traveled ahead, while he followed a while later. When I visited the doctor at the resort, he made me aware that I had an inflammation in the nose. I had previously seen a specialist in Posen, who prescribed some salve for its care. The doctor at the resort suggested that I undergo an operation at the resort to correct this inflammation. I declined this suggestion and, when Father joined me at the resort, he agreed with my decision. On the way back we stopped in Berlin. There, I was advised to see Professor Lasser. When he saw me he confirmed the need to have the operation and so I underwent it in his clinic. After a few days, I was released from there and went to stay with the children. Dr. Lasser cleared me only at the beginning of September. It was awful to cope with the curious looks of the people in Graetz, who were looking at my disfigured nose. One gets used to everything, and so I too overcame the looks at my nose.

On September 25 [*1899*], our children [*Hedwig and Julius*] in Berlin welcomed their first child, our second grandchild, who was given the name Fritz [*Friedrich Samuel Brodnitz, 1899–1995*]. As I still was recovering and needed some rest, Rosa came to help Hedwig during her recovery. As a result of this, Father and I only came to Berlin for the *brit*. This led to a festive occasion in which the Brodnitz and Herzfeld families gathered together. The youngster thrived well, and during the summer of the year 1900, we were able to welcome both grandchildren in Graetz [*Fritz Brodnitz and Kurt Meyer from Stargard*].

In the middle of July, Father went with me to Reichenhall. This visit was not very successful, and in late fall I went again for consultation to Dr. Gerhard in Berlin. He claimed to find something in the larynges and suggested that I go to a throat specialist. A visit to Professor Frankel in Berlin led to a suggestion that the lungs were infected. He recommended that I go for a longer stay in Reiboldsgroen or Falkenstein. This was also suggested by our family doctor. I returned home and, at the suggestion of Dr. Rubensohn, I went to see Dr. Cassel in Posen. He too recommended that I go to Falkenstein. After lengthy consideration, I went there at the middle of April 1901.

In April of 1899, Hugo had transferred to Darmstadt in order to study at the Higher Electric School. Now he came to Frankfurt am Main, and on the following day we traveled to Falkenstein. As hard as the decision was to come to this resort, the first days there were even more difficult. Only after fourteen days, when Hugo joined me, did I finally become acclimated a bit to the place. A Mrs. Trusch, who was also a patient at the clinic, was warm and full of good humor. A Mrs. Professor Jahn from Bernburg, who was at my table during the meals, also became friendly. Having Hugo as guest on weekends also gave me reason to feel hope and joy. After the first fourteen days, when my temperature returned to a normal level, I was given permission to go on hikes. Mrs. Trusch was ready to join me. As she also took a liking to Hugo, we became ever closer as companions.

Father had gone to Wiesbaden in July. I was very happy when I could pick him up from Cronberg. Our days together passed in a great hurry. I would have liked to go back home with him, but the doctors insisted that it was too early for me to go, and they felt that this would endanger my recovery.

I had spent four-and-one-half months in that recovery, and only in September, because of the coming holidays, did the doctors agree to have me leave the place. They had me promise that I would continue my care while back at home. This I did, and the results were very good for a long period of time.

While I was away, Bianka took care of the household. Father was very satisfied with her handling of the house, and Aunts Stern and Badt, who had come for visits to Graetz while I was away, also reported that all went so well that one hardly noticed my absence from the house. This was more than I could have expected from such a young girl.

A short time after I had returned home, Lenchen came for a visit and informed us that she was expecting a second child. Hedwig was also expecting, and so we faced the happy prospect of doubling the number of our grandchildren. At the suggestion of Mrs. Lipschitz, I hired a Mrs. Fleischer as a helper in the house. Before she got married, this woman had been a helper in the Brodnitz household for many years. I was not supposed to undertake the household work, and we wanted to enable Bianka to go on visits to her sisters.

I forgot to mention that Bianka, our last child, was sent during the fall of 1899 to Mrs. Silbermann's care in Berlin. The circumcision of our grandson Fritz provided us with the opportunity to accompany Bianka to Berlin. She stayed there for nearly one year. As the boarding house had become smaller by that time, it allowed Mrs. S. to dedicate more of her time to each resident. Bianka gained more from her stay and was able to develop many lasting friendships. This was aided by the fact that she could frequently visit with her married sister, who was living in the city. Hedwig and Julius took great care of Bianka, and she spent many stimulating Sundays with them. The little nephew Fritz, in whom Bianka found special joy, was also an attraction for her.

The many hours that Bianka had spent in Berlin with music and painting developed her interest in these subjects. Upon her return home, we gladly let her continue both of these studies. She had to travel to Posen once each week for these lessons. This also brought her in closer contact with the family members who lived in Posen. In the fall of 1901, in recognition of her efforts while I was recovering in Falkenstein, we allowed her to spend several weeks in Posen. At that time Ernst and Hermann were in Posen, as trainees. They were frequently at the home of the Brodnitz siblings. At that time the affectionate relationship between the third Brodnitz and the third Herzfeld, led to renewed ties between the two families. Both Ernst and Hermann had spent a year of military service with the field artillery unit in Posen. They also worked as trainees in Schneidemuehl and later in Posen. The proximity allowed them to come for frequent Sundays to Graetz. Hugo and Rosa also came frequently on Sundays for visits to us, which always resulted in festivities for all.

Our third grandchild, named Otto, was born on December 24, 1901. On New Year's Eve we traveled to Berlin, to be present at the *brit,* which took place on New Year's Day, 1902. Once again, Rosa rushed to Berlin to be of help to her sister and run Hedwig's household. Hugo followed her in time for the circumcision. As was the case earlier, when Fritz was born, Julius' siblings who were living in Berlin, as well as Hermann and Ernst, who came especially from Posen, all joined in the festivities.

We stayed in Berlin for a few extra days and enjoyed to see that Fritz was already developing well and showed signs that he would become an intelligent young fellow.

Winter passed slowly and on March 29, 1902, our fourth grandson was born in Stargard. He was given the name Walter [*Walter Mayer*]. Father and I traveled also to this circumcision. Rosa rushed again to help her sister Lenchen run the household after the birth.

Both Otto in Berlin and Walter in Stargard were developing slowly. Lenchen was breast-feeding, while Otto was fed from a bottle. Hedwig had endless problems with this child and had to spend much effort to bring him through his first year. During a visit to them in the summer of the year 1902, the child looked so weak and unhealthy that I left with a heavy heart, fearing that I might never get to see him again. Lenchen too suffered through a difficult year with her second child. To our great joy, both developed rather well after that first period.

In the meantime, Ernst had completed his trainee period and took his Assessor's test in the fall of the year 1902. He was notified in January of 1903 that he had passed the test. After the tests, he took over the practice of a lawyer by the name of Dr. Kaempfer in Posen, while that man went on his honeymoon. Ernst also used this time to investigate where he should settle down. Both his father and I had wished that he would settle in Berlin. Ernst was not so inclined and was supported in that opinion by Julius, who told him that he did not believe that it would be easy to establish a meaningful legal office in Berlin. He believed that it might take a long while to get such a place going. As Ernst did not wish to live on Father's handouts, he did not think that this was a good idea. A letter from a friend of the children, by the name of Mr. Ernst Hirsch, who was living in Berlin, drew such a very enticing picture of the possibilities for a career for a young man in the city of Essen. That caused Ernst to declare that he wished to see this Promised Land for himself in order to form his own judgment. He traveled to Essen, and after a few days he wrote to us that he did, indeed, consider the possibilities in Essen to be very inviting. He asked for our permission to settle in Essen. This was not an easy decision for us. We had already had the intention to move from Graetz to Berlin, and it would have been much better for us had Ernst settled in that city. We figured, however, that someone as thoughtful and serious as Ernst could best judge what was right for him and that we should not stand in his way or disturb his plans. Father, therefore, gave his reluctant approval to Ernst's plans. Thanks to God that Ernst never had to regret his decision, and while we often wished that he lived nearer to us, we had to admit that it would have been most unlikely for him to have had such a successful position in such a short time anywhere else. One had to accept the fact that one had to rely on written communication with each other. Saturdays, the day when his weekly report arrived, became for us the day to which we were looking forward to all week long.

In March of that year, Hermann also passed his examination and shortly thereafter reported to work at his brother-in-law Meyer's place in Danzig, where they had been waiting for him for quite a while. Now the two close friends, who had been together since high school days and who studied together and were together in the military service, became separated, with one in the East and the other in the West of the country. However, the distance in places of residence did not impact the lasting friendship. During their first vacation, they and their friend Galland, who had in the meantime settled in Posen, met in Helgoland. Father and I went in that same summer on vacation to Heringsdorf. From there, we went for a few days to Copenhagen, on my first sea voyage, which turned out to be a complete success. Hugo was at our home during that time. He and Bianka took care of the business and the house in our absence.

In Copenhagen we visited Glyptotek and the Thorwaldsen Museum, City Hall, and other public buildings, all of which were worth seeing. We also visited the sea resorts at Klampenborg and Skodoborg, traveled through the wonderful Eremitage forests, etc., as well as to the castle of Frederiksborg and its gardens. We spent an evening at the Tivoli Park, which, truth be told, we expected to be more than it really was. We also took a tour through the harbor. On our trip back, we traveled by ship from Malmo to Sassnitz in stormy weather. Although the ship was rather large, three-quarters of all the passengers on board the ship became ill. Both of us remained well, and we landed toward evening in Sassnitz, where we spent the night. In the afternoon we traveled to Kaiserstuhl and enjoyed viewing the forests along the way. The next morning we traveled back to Heringsdorf on a beautiful new ship by the name of "Odu."

In the fall of that year, Father talked me into joining him on a trip to Berlin where he had to be for a meeting of the board of directors of the association of building block manufacturers. From Berlin, Father went to visit Ernst in Essen, as he wanted to get a feel for the place. He returned rather satisfied. Ernst had already a fair amount of work, and the social circles in which he found himself seemed to Father to be very satisfactory. When Ernst came to visit us at New Year's time, we learned enough to accept that the move to this faraway location was justified.

In the meantime, Hermann established his career in Danzig to the point that he could now realize his wish to get married. We had assumed for quite a while now that there was much affection between him and Bianka. During the course of a visit that Bianka made to her siblings in Berlin in January 1904, Hermann also came to that city. We were surprised to receive a telegram from them, in which they had asked for our approval to their engagement. We were glad and happy to do so, and a week later they got engaged in the presence of the lovely guests, who came for the event from Posen, Berlin, and Stargard.

Hermann wanted to have the wedding set for an early date. When he came to visit during Easter, the date was fixed for May 15. That meant that we had to hurry up with the purchases. This required a few trips to Posen and one trip to Berlin. I went with Bianka to Berlin, where we completed the bulk of the purchases. I left Bianka with Hedwig to purchase the rest while I returned home.

I was rather sick during that period and had to throw up frequently. As a consequence of that, the frequent trips, during which I could not live by a predictable schedule, were very hard on me.

The wedding was planned to take place in Posen, while the civil marriage was to take place in Graetz. The new mayor of Graetz, Mr. Howe, was kind enough to schedule the civil ceremony for Ascension Day. Hugo Brodnitz and Ernst came for this occasion and were very jolly during the dinner that followed it. On Friday we traveled together to Posen where the actual ceremony took place on Sunday. Rabbi Krakauer from Breslau came to officiate. The whole Brodnitz clan that had come for the occasion stated that this was the nicest wedding of the three that the Herzfelds had arranged. As an aside, this was also the most expensive of the three, in spite of the fact that fewer people participated in this wedding than were present at the wedding of Rosa and Hugo.

I felt rather sick during the wedding but kept it to myself, as I did not want to disrupt the event and also did not want to cause Bianka to be concerned when she went away. Once it was over, I collapsed and I had to be seen and treated by Dr. Korach, in

Posen. He determined that I suffered from a gastric trouble and ordered me to take four weeks of bed rest, during which I was restricted to taking only liquid meals. These meals were strictly prescribed in terms of quantities and timing. Following this period, the physician told me to go to a Dr. Pariser, who ran a sanitarium in Homburg.

When Hedwig learned about my situation, she came to Graetz to take care of me and provide me company. She then arranged that after fourteen days, Lenchen replaced her. Lenchen came with little Walter, who helped me pass the time.

Because of the pending wedding of our nephew Albert Badt, which was to take place in Darmstadt, Father was forced to go there earlier than I could go with him. I also did not want him to have to travel back and forth this great distance three times in a short period of time. He therefore went to Homburg, where he could take part in a restful stay. He stayed in a house not far from Dr. Pariser. He was then able to meet me for the trip to Frankfurt. My stay in Homburg did help me get much better. Under the care of Dr. Pariser, I was able to gain ten pounds during the four weeks that I had stayed there.

Ernst and Hugo came to visit us frequently. The former surprised us when he informed us that he wanted to get married and asked for our consent before he entered into a serious relationship with the girl of his choice. Both Father and I had some doubts, which caused us to hold back our consent. Father wanted to check out her family background, while I had the fear that as a result of such a marriage, Ernst would be lost to us, as the young lady and her family came from a completely different background than our family. Ernst knew how to set aside all our concerns and as a matter of fact, we received her as an additional daughter, who is as close to us as one of our own children [*this was Klara Frankensein, the mother of Julius, Walter, Hanna, and Chava*].

After Father obtained very good information about the family from several sources, Ernst traveled to Baden-Baden, where the young lady's family was on vacation. On the day before our departure from Homburg, we received a telegram that the couple got engaged. They wanted to come and visit us in Homburg, but we proposed to meet the following day, undisturbed, in Frankfurt, whereupon Klara's mother accompanied them on their trip to that city. That evening the three of them traveled back to Karlsruhe, while we returned home on the next morning. It was very nice for both sides to get to know one another in this way. For me it was especially good to see that Ernst was so happy.

Left to right, back: Hugo Brodnitz, Hermann Brodnitz; front: Julie Herzfeld, Bianka Brodnitz; photo likely from the early 1900s

We only spent one night in Berlin on our return trip, as Julius and Hedwig were at that time away on a trip.

The wedding was set for the first day of Christmas in Frankfurt am Main. We came to Karlsruhe ahead of time for the civil marriage, as we wanted to get to know the environment from which our daughter-in-law was coming. Klara's mother, grandparents, and siblings all impressed us as nice people.

The wedding followed on the first day of Christmas, in Frankfurt. All our children showed up, except for Hedwig and Bianka, who were not allowed to travel as they were in special circumstances [*late pregnancies*].

The festivities were very nice and pleasant. A few days later, we traveled back to Graetz via Berlin with the children who lived in Posen, Julius and Hermann.

The plan was to move to Berlin on April 1. We had already rented a flat in Berlin and had sold the three properties that we had in Graetz. During the months of January and February, we had made all the preparations for the move. That was a major project, as we had to get rid of all that had accumulated in the house over all these many years. We also had to review all the business-related documents, a task that Father assigned to me.

A portion of the furniture had to be given away, and I located willing recipients for it. In March I traveled once again to Berlin to make all the necessary arrangements. I obtained window treatments for the flat, as well as purchased the needed carpets, etc., so that all could be quickly arranged once we made our move.

During our departure we saw how much love and respect we had enjoyed in our old hometown. From all sides, we were told how sorry they were to see us leave Graetz. They went overboard in farewells of all kinds. Father was given the title of honorable citizen of the town by the municipal authorities and the town's council. The Jewish community named Father as an honorary member and the Jewish Women's Organization also made me an honorary member. The Organization of German Women gave me a nice going away party as well as a vase made of Royal Tin, with flowers. We were both pleased by the sentiment shown to us.

On April 1, we received the news from our children in Berlin that the third youngster had arrived [*Heinz Brodnitz, my father, 1905–1984*]. This time Rosa could not rush to help, as she was waiting for an equally happy occasion to take place in Danzig.

On April 10, we left our lovely Graetz. Once again many friends accompanied us to the railroad station. Loaded down with all the flowers that were given to me, we left our old home to the new destination in full anticipation of living closer to the children and to our siblings. During our last period in Graetz, after all the children had left, we felt rather alone in that place.

Our dear Lenchen came to Berlin to help us move and arrange the flat. On the day of the move, I developed a bad backache and could not move. I could, therefore, also not attend the *brit* of our young grandchild, who was given the name Heinz. On April 12, little Kaethe [*daughter of Herman and Bianka Brodnitz*] arrived in Danzig, and I must confess that I was especially pleased to have a girl as grandchild after having already five grandsons.

For the Easter holidays, our apartment was finished and both of us felt good in the new surroundings. The distance to the children's place was small, according to the standards of Berlin, so that one is able to get together frequently. The grandchildren were a special pleasure, as they developed nicely in both body and mind. As we had a small garden in our new place, both Fritz and Otto had a small plot in which they planted and cared for some vegetation.

We went to Wiesbaden in early May, where we met with the Badt siblings who lived in Glogau. We spent several nice weeks together, until I suddenly developed a painful inflammation on the skin of my breasts. The local doctor did not know what to do, but it was suggested that I undergo an operation to remove it. I preferred to return to Berlin to continue there with the treatment. When they operated, it turned out to be the correct thing to do. Ten days after the operation, I was fully recovered.

In early July, Father went to Graetz to a meeting of the supervisory board. When he came back, he reported that he no longer felt a close connection to the place. He said that under no circumstances would he be interested in moving back to that town. This news removed a large stone from my heart because I always feared that living in Berlin, without a full-time occupation, would be a problem for Father. I was doubly happy to learn that he really felt well in this new place.

The first holder of the Herzfeld family name was born in Essen on October 6, 1905. He was given the name Julius. Both of us traveled to the *brit*. We were pleased to see and to hear how well Ernst's office had developed and how happy he was living with his wife. During the following summer both came to us for a visit. We also met the children who lived in Danzig during a summer vacation in Zoppot. This gave us a chance to get to know their little one. It was a rather pleasant stay there, as Hedwig and her three children also came to that place on vacation and Julius also came to there.

We spent a very pleasant first winter in Berlin, and I was at that time in rather good health. As a result, we were able to subscribe to a series of concerts, which gave me much pleasure. We also attended the theater rather frequently, something that we could not do while living in Graetz. It now gave us much joy to be able to do that.

The old problems with my digestion reoccurred from time to time, causing me to suffer from pain and causing me to have to throw up. The doctors treated it as a case of gallstones and ordered me to go to Karlsbad for a treatment. For the first time, Father accompanied me on this visit. He did not stay for the whole period of the treatment as he had to go to Kiel to attend a meeting of the delegates of the building block trade organization. The stay in Karlsbad during April and May had done little to improve my condition and so the doctors suggested that I go in July to a sanitarium near Schlachtensee, where I had to rest a lot in the open air. This treatment also did not help much, and so we decided to go south in the winter. Shortly before we left, our children [*Julius and Hedwig with their children*] moved to the apartment on Schillerstrasse. The move took place on a day when all of Berlin was covered with snow. While the move was taking place, the youngsters were with us, which was a great pleasure for us.

We left Berlin on February 5. The side streets were covered with mountains of snow, as it took a lot of work to remove all this snow.

Notes

Julie Badt Herzfeld was born on November 25, 1848, in Graefenhain, Germany, and died July 11, 1914, in Berlin, Germany.

She was the mother of
- Max (Meschulem) Herzfeld (1868–1872)
- Louis (Leib) Herzfeld (1869–1870)
- Rosa Herzfeld Brodnitz (1871–1932)
- Helene (Lenchen) Herzfeld Meyer (1873–?)
- Ernst Solomon Herzfeld (1875–1948)
- Emma (Ester) Herzfeld (1876–1877)
- Hedwig Herzfeld Brodnitz (1878–1938)
- Betty Herzfeld (1880)
- Hugo Herzfeld (1881–1933)
- Bianka Herzfeld Brodnitz (1883–?)

The original manuscript of Julie's memoir.

Chapter 2
Julius Brodnitz

Dictated and transcribed as
noted in 1926.

A miniature copy of the portrait of
Dr. Julius Brodnitz, painted by Prof.
Erich Wolfsfeld in 1926

As I LOOK BACK at the sixty years of my life that have now been almost completed, rather than using the common saying that I wandered through life, I can instead say that my whole existence was formed at my parents' house. It was not only a source of memories but also a life that created life.

My hometown, Posen [*Polish spelling, Poznan*], which has since then been unfortunately removed by brute force from the German Fatherland [*in 1918*], was a solid, middle-class town. It was not a place with a very high intellectual quotient, but, at least as far as its Jewish population was concerned, a standard level was reached.

My father, Samuel Brodnitz, came from a well-respected family originating from the small town of Schwersenz [*now called Swarzedz, 8 km east of Posen, Poland*] near Posen. Schwersenz was

---

Note from Julius: I am dictating these notes without any supporting material, solely from my memories, while Master Wolfsfeld is painting me.

almost exclusively inhabited by Jews. Their justified claim was that those Jews who did not want to be isolated in the Posner Ghetto [*Ghetto of Posen*] had settled in that town. The Jews in Schwersenz achieved a freer status within their community. However, even in Schwersenz, the Jews were categorized as *Schützjuden*. That meant that the Jews were protected (*geschützt*) when the Jewish community accepted a person to live amongst them. The acceptance was achieved via the receipt of a Jewish letter of citizenship [*Burgerbrief*]. As a child in Posen, I had often heard from families who had obtained such letters from my grandfather, Leib Brodnitz. He, as chairperson of the community, had signed them.

Many well-known Jewish families originated from Schwersenz. Many of those who rose to the top ranks of German-Jewish life came from Posen and were from families that originated in Schwersenz.

My grandfather [*Leib*] was born [*in 1792*] before Southern Prussia, which included the province of Posen, was acquired [*by Germany*]. It is noteworthy that he received basically a German education. He was able to write in perfect German. This was a rarity at that time. Think for example about the battles that Moses Mendelssohn endured when he attempted to give the Jews of his time the benefit of a German education. The explanation of this difference rests in the fact that in Posen there was an early push to obtain a German education.

Characteristically, when the famous Rabbi Akiva Eger was summoned to Posen at the beginning of the nineteenth century, there was serious concern that he would clash with those families that elected to educate their children in the German language. The archives of Posen contain a letter from the Posner Jewish community and the Prussian government. This letter is unsigned, as the community leaders state that they were afraid, lest Rabbi Akiva Eger, if appointed to the pulpit, would use it to curse them. In his contract it is stated that the Rabbi committed himself not to attack from his podium those who elected to give their children a modern education. He also agreed not to agitate wives against husbands or children against parents. When one reads such documents, one must wonder that my grandfather, a Jew, was able to enjoy such a German education in the eighteenth century.

According to what my grandfather said, however, the explanation was as follows: only a few regular schools as we know them today were available to the general public at that time. The Jewish desire to obtain an education led to the Jewish custom that, ever since long ago, those who had achieved a higher level of education were held in highest esteem, even when they were relatively poor. Characteristically, we find in many fields people who dedicated their time to the study of a profession. Such a young student, known as a *Bocher*, was supported in his studies by a number of families.

This young student was provided room, clothing, and board. He showed his appreciation to the supporting families by teaching their children. As there was no fixed curriculum, it depended on the *Bocher* which skills he taught the children.

It was surely not by chance that my grandfather's parents selected to support a *Bocher* who could read and write German and who taught the children to read and write in German.

My grandfather already carried the name Brodnitz. From my father and from my grandmother I heard that it was only by chance that we were given this name. An edict was issued that all the Jews had to choose civilian names. The Jewish circles did not consider this edict significant. One went by the name of one's father. When Schul ben Leib [*Hebrew for "Schul, son of Leib"*] had a civil name entered into the governmental list, it would be without changing his current designation. The authorities had set a deadline for the selection of new family names.

On the day at which the new name had to be reported, my great-grandfather [*the father of Leib Brodnitz*] was on a journey. He apparently gave the selection of a new name so little attention that he left no instructions with his wife. When the local official came to inquire, my great-grandmother could only tell him that the great-grandfather was in Brodnica [*probably the town 30 km south of Posen*] but had not selected a name. The official, therefore, wrote down Brodnica on his list.

My grandfather was a youth when the French invaded Posen and Schwersenz. I inherited his silver tobacco box with the picture of General Baron Chassé that was given to the young man by a French officer [*this box is still in our family's possession*].

My father was given a solid German education. During his youth, he was also taught by a Jewish teacher by the name of Merzbach. This teacher was still teaching at the *Buergerschule* [*"townspeople's school," that is, a school that was not run by a religious group*] during my school days.

My father had also been given a full Hebrew education. Not only did he possess an empirical knowledge of Hebrew, but I had seen in his small library a book of Hebrew grammar. He also had a good basic knowledge of the Talmud. It was a great joy to attend services with him at the synagogue, where he provided me with the historic and linguistic background of the prayers. My father also studied French and read classic French books. He also possessed a broad knowledge of the works of classic German writers, which he absorbed with much interest. I remember several occasions where he talked with enthusiasm about these classic writers, during which he also quoted from their works. He pointed out to me that, as one reads and rereads these classical works, they gain a new meaning at each age.

My father belonged to the admired generation that combined the values of the old ghetto life with modern culture. In his total outlook, he was what is known today as a "German Jew." The educated Jews of Posen believed in a noble and pure patriotism. Because of the conservatism of their inherited background, they tended to support the parties that leaned politically to the right. My father supported the direction of the Lasker-Bennigsen movement [*Eduard Lasker (1829–1884) and Rudolf von Bennigsen (1824–1902) were German politicians who were active in the National Liberal Party*]. In my youth, during the period after the Great War of 1870 [*French-German War*], there was a frictionless relationship between the Jews of Posen and the local officials. This changed only after the appearance of Treitschke and Stoecker [*Heinrich von Treitschke (1834–1896) and Adolf Stoecker (1835–1909) were early anti-Semitic politicians in Germany in the 1870s*]. I recall that during that period, a member of the *Fortschritts Partei* [*Progress Party*] became the candidate in the Prussian elections. My father debated at great length before deciding to bolt from the National-Liberal Party and to support the *Fortschritts* group. Personal experience played a role in these decisions.

My brother Felix, who unfortunately died at an early age [*twenty-four*], was, in the years 1879 to 1880, a junior barrister in Posen. He volunteered for a year of military service in the 6th Regiment. According to the regulations of that time, in order to become a candidate for an officer's rank, he had to be awarded the so-called Buttons, as a noncommissioned officer. He was, without a doubt, a capable soldier who fulfilled all his required tasks. In fact, he paid with his life for carrying out his duty. He became sick during some exercise but thought that it was his military obligation to take part in the summer field exercises, as he would otherwise not be considered for advancement. I remember that my father contacted his friends in both Jewish and Christian circles, but my brother's promotion did not take place. As small as it may appear, that experience caused my father and many Jews in respected positions to separate from the National Liberal Party.

My father was a businessman to the core. The story of his company, which was always held in high regard, was one of steady, rather than sudden, growth. He always moved forward. His activities as a businessman were notable in two ways.

In all of his business dealings, which he pursued with all his energy, he never crossed the line that would have collided with his solid values. I remember discussions in my parents' house of numerous business projects that would have considerably expanded the basis of the business. My father was proud that he always had at his disposal the means to fulfill his obligations and that he never had to worry about how he would satisfy his undertakings. Moreover, he was careful to make sure that his financial resources were always sufficient to take care of all possible changing situations. Characteristically, never in his life did he have to sign a bill of exchange [*mortgage*].

The second characteristic feature of my father's personality as a businessman was his pride in his profession. He was very aware that he, to the extent of his ability and resources, was part of a big economic organism. He felt that he deserved respect only as long as his activities reflected this responsibility.

Upon coming home, my father seldom if ever talked about business. Such a balance was only possible because of his generous outlook on life. My father certainly did not scorn economic success, but it did not affect the content of his life. The content of his life was based on his family. The family was the essence of all his thoughts. I often heard him say that a certain proposed new business opportunity looked appealing but that he had to think about his family and, therefore, had to turn down any business that had a speculative character. In this striving, he had my mother's full support [*Rosalie Weissbein*].

Berlin, June 28, 1926

My mother came from a respected family from Bromberg [*Bydgoszcz, Poland, 107 km northeast of Posen*]. Her father, Heimann Weissbein, was a cherry brandy maker and the owner of a fur store. I have always identified myself to friends as a descendent, on my mother's side, of a workman. Workmen were, at least in

Rosalie Weissbein Brodnitz and Samuel Brodnitz, likely in the 1870s

Germany, a rarity among the Jews. It gave me satisfaction to hear how this workman achieved fortune and respect through honest hard work.

When one talks about fortune, one must not think in terms of the period before the war [*World War I*]. My mother was considered to be a very rich young lady because her father gave her, as a dowry, 4,000 Talers [*a Taler was a silver coin, roughly equal in size to a silver dollar*] in addition to a great number of silk dresses and furs.

I inherited my white hair from my grandfather. For as long as I can remember both my grandfather Weissbein and my grandmother had white hair. I only remember that when Grandfather Weissbein died, my grandmother gave each of us some fur collars, fur hats, etc. from his store. My grandmother [*Weissbein*] was especially attached to my father, who provided her and her children with good advice. I remember as characteristic that when there was even the most minor disagreement between my mother and my father, Grandmother Weissbein always sided with my father [*her son-in-law*]. This was clearly a sign of lifelong experience and wisdom.

I still remember with joy the days I spent in the Bromberg house [*Bromberg was the town where Grandmother Weissbein had lived*] after the death of my brother Felix in 1880. Grandmother made a special effort to make the stay of her relatives as nice as possible.

She made a special effort to meet all her obligations so that during our stay she never had to be embarrassed by difficulties. She, therefore, received each visitor with the strange question: "Dear child, you know how much I love you. But please do tell me, how long are you going to stay?" This was said in such a friendly manner that it could not possibly lead to a misunderstanding. May I just add that whenever I was amongst my relatives in Bromberg, there was always a beautiful sense of belonging.

My uncle Louis Jacoby was especially proud of two things: first that his family was the first Jewish family that was permitted to settle in Bromberg and second that no one won the title of *schutzen konig* [*king of the sharp shooters*] as often as he did. In his home, there was a wall filled with medals awarded to him during sharp-shooting contests. The members of the Weissbein and Jacoby families met in the evening and often also in the afternoon by the bench at the old distillation, vinegar, and liquor factory of J. L. Jacoby, named *Zum Lachs* ["*To the Salmon*"], at the Friedrich Circle. The dignified and much-loved uncle and his splendid wife, Aunt Johanna Jacoby, who in all respects, including her appearance, was most similar to my mother, were a dignified couple, of the Biedermeier character [*at the time, referencing a solid yet satirical imaginary German bourgeois figure, "Gottlieb Biedermeier"; now a term sometimes used to describe German and Austrian art and architecture between the Congress of Vienna (1815) and the Revolution of 1848*]. They had modest needs and were happy with their lot. Their values were especially noted when the uncle died at an early age, and the aunt not only was able to run the business and to provide for her children, but was also able to continue to develop this enterprise.

I have just noticed that my memories failed me. I lived at the Jacoby's but was so frequently at my grandmother's place that I can hardly separate the two places in my memories.

My mother was a very special person, in her simplicity and naturalness. She certainly was lucky in her life. In my whole life

I have seldom met a woman who, with full justification, was as proud of her man as she was. Starting from modest circumstances in 1848, my father built up his grain business so that it was respected far beyond the borders of his hometown or his home province. She welcomed this success, but she never considered it as something relevant to her joy in life. She looked at the fortune that my father eventually accumulated only as an assurance that she could bring up her children as she wished in her heart. From my mother's mouth, which never uttered empty sayings, I often heard that one only has a fortune to allow parents to leave it to their offspring, that is, to get an education that will provide them with security.

My father and mother complemented each other in a most lucky way. My father was essentially a very serious man who internalized everything and took it very seriously. My mother had a happy nature with confidence in her expressions that often bordered on those of a young fellow. My father took the occasion of any failing on our part as a cause for a lengthy speech. These speeches were interrupted by my mother saying: "Why are you talking your lungs out? Just give the boy a spanking." To the best of my recollections, my father never followed my mother's advice. My mother claimed that, in the case of one of the older siblings, she herself executed this punishment. My eldest brother Hugo confirmed this claim and stated that he had his hair pulled so frequently that it caused him to get bald at an early age. Later in life, my mother developed a proprietary executive method to mete out punishment: When things got out of hand among my younger siblings, my elder brother Alfons was summoned as he had the position of enforcer. He appeared in the house, which was next to the store, to carry out the punishment, accompanied by Mother, who claimed to be too weak to do so herself. (P.S. These penalties, even when carried out by my brother in a reinforced fashion, never harmed anyone.) Personally, I was already too old when this punitive system was introduced. I do not seem to remember being castigated by my mother. I also have my doubts as to whether or not she had the energy to carry out such punishment even at an earlier time.

When I stated above that my mother came near to having youthful expressions, I meant to illustrate the relationship between my mother and her children. We never felt embarrassed in our relationship with her. Never during my years as a child and even as a youngster did I feel that I could not have Mother as a confidante.

It was characteristic of my mother that when I left home to go to the university, she gave me the following advice: "Young man, do not get into debt. If, however, you do get into debt, get the loan from me." I followed this suggestion, in a moderate fashion. Actually, mostly when I could not manage on my monthly students' allowance, I did not have to write. There must have been a mental connection between my mother and me. Whenever I was running short of funds a package arrived. On the package it was written that in the socks there was a 10 or 20 Mark coin. I was not to confirm the arrival of the money to my father. It was enough if I wrote that the socks arrived in good shape.

My mother, who gave birth to twelve children and was able to bring up nine of them, was overwhelmed by the responsibilities of the household. Except for Saturdays and on a holiday, Mother was always busy but never complained, except in pretense or in jest. She never wanted to have anything else in her life. She said, "If I ever stop working, then want and misery will be followed by death."

In consequence of the extraordinarily free contact between our mother and her children, Mother also took an active role in our spiritual development. She was an avid reader who read much and with great pleasure. She always read the books that we had recommended to her. She loved to go to bed early after a hard day's work and read in bed for hours on end. She always got great pleasure out of approaching each book with an unbiased but natural criticism. Only very seldom did she make pronouncements about a book that were, according to my judgment, not exactly to the point. It is interesting to note that this very typical middle-class woman allowed us to recommend to her reading material about people from other classes or circumstances. During my days as a student, my mother enjoyed going to see performances of French morality and other plays. It was very funny to hear her exclaim: "Believe me, this is how life really is." I never found out what gave her this positive point of view. I can only assume that in this aspect too, she expressed her pride in her husband, who was, according to her, completely different from most other men.

In my parents' house, things were never luxurious. On the other hand, there was never any shortage. According to today's standards, Mother purchased extremely large quantities. Of course, she had good and long-standing relations with the various sales people. Twice per week the so-called Jewish Miss—that is how our maid announced her—came from the Schwersenz market to deliver the bulk of the households' needs. According to all measures, these orders were very generous. Specific quantities were never mentioned. Instead my mother ordered "a meal's worth of fish" or "a large hen." Payment followed according to custom or sheet, not according to weight or measure.

In contrast to my father, my mother lacked the presentation skills. She had little sense for levity. And yet, the evenings at my parents' home were filled with dignity that made itself noted even in the presence of six young boys and three girls.

I note with special thanks the fact that I came from a family that was rich in children. Each of us went his or her own way. It was characteristic that none of the nine siblings had friends in common. Only a household full of children educates one to be independent and have a sense of responsibility. This showed itself in the way elder siblings took up the responsibility for the younger ones. Above all, my eldest brother, Hugo, joined Father's business early on and quickly became the source of Father's pride. While my brother's business initiatives were sharply curbed in accordance with Father's basic rules for the business, Father soon handed over to Hugo most of the daily responsibilities, although Father continued to be involved in the business to the end of his life.

I believe that when one of my brother's initiatives failed to work out, Father never complained about the young ones who think they know everything better. He had a good understanding for the feeling of responsibility of his son and did not want to make it harder on him than it was already.

Both of my parents had a special love for my Brodnitz grandparents. Nonetheless, it is characteristic that my mother never addressed my grandfather in the familiar pronoun *(Du)* but instead addressed him using the respectful form *(Sie)*.

These Brodnitz grandparents [*Julius' grandparents, Leib and Caroline*] deserve further mention in these *Memories*.

Grandfather was a man of noticeable high stature, with a face that was shaven clean, except for his so-called *Zimmermanns-fraese*, that is, with the body of a beard below the chin. My grandmother was a smaller, stocky woman with the appearance of someone with a wooden knee. Grandfather looked like the typical older farmer. Over the years he probably left most of the problems of the household to my grandmother. As I mentioned before, Grandfather was the supervisor of the Schwersenz community, where the rest of his family had also resided. I remember, for instance, that there was a Brodnitz Hotel in Schwersenz, which was founded by his brother. He retired with a fortune that would probably only be equal to a year's salaries of modest civil servants. At first he participated in the businesses of his sons. With time, he limited his involvement to providing some of his meager capital to his sons at a rather high interest. Although my grandparents considered themselves as solidly middle class, their lifestyle was so

Leib Brodnitz (1792–1893), taken in the 1880s in Posen

frugal that we can hardly appreciate it these days. My grandparents lived in an apartment that consisted of only two rooms and a kitchen. Grandmother had no household help until she was well over eighty years old.

Of the two rooms, one was a living room, which was furnished with light colored pine furniture. All the walls were covered with pictures. Whenever someone in the wider family circle obtained new photographic pictures, one copy was given to the grandparents. Framing these many pictures would have resulted in cost that could not be paid with their meager means had Grandmother not made a very successful purchase of a big lot of oval frames. This lot took care of the needs of our growing family until Grandmother's death.

Candles were the only source of light in their house. A pair of large oil lamps that were in the room was no longer in use. When we visited the grandparents as children, these lamps only served as a source of amusement for us, as raising and lowering the wick was funny and caused a gurgling sound.

The only luxurious items in the living room were the many small figurines made of porcelain that stood on the large table in this room. When the grandparents were alone at home, they put out the candles, as they felt that light was not needed to hold a conversation.

Not only during holidays but also every Saturday, the family gathered at noon in the grandparent's place. This clearly says a lot, as my father's sisters also had unusually large families. Nonetheless, there was always some so-called crumbly cake for all who came.

My eldest brother brought special friends to this reception so that they could share in this blessed event.

How my grandmother managed with her meager means is still a puzzle for me. My grandfather gave her the "princely" amount of 6 Taler per week, and Grandmother complained that her husband expected unrealistic food to be provided with this budget. Grandfather complained that a friend of his also gave his wife 6 Taler per week but that this friend got to eat a roasted duck twice per week. Nonetheless, Grandmother still had some money for other occasions. She had a great circle of people who were in need and she was able to support them, even if only by giving them a few Groschen [*pennies*], which also came from her 6 Talers allowance. I can hardly remember a time when Grandmother came to visit when her big bag did not contain a small gift for each of the children, even if it was only a pretty pencil. We welcomed Grandmother and her large bag with such excitement that our mother often called out to us to be careful not to knock Grandmother off her feet.

Besides the story about the origin of the family name, I have been able to learn only very little about the history of my grandfather's family. It is probably typical that my grandfather could not provide me with any further details about the family history. My grandmother came from the Holz family. The recently deceased Privy Council Holz and his brother, attorney Holz, were descendants of this family. My grandmother boasted that she originated from an old family of rabbis. I was unable to learn more about this claim. She only told me that my uncle, Nehemias Brodnitz, was named after a rabbi, from whom she was a descendant [*in other words, Nehemias was named after someone on Grandma Brodnitz's or the Holz side of the family*].

My grandmother was deeply devoted. One could certainly say that she was chopped of the wood of which martyrs are cut [*"holz" means "wood" in German*]. This rather uncomplicated woman was able to develop at the moment of need an internal fortitude that one would never have expected from her. I have often retold of the time when I went to her just before I started my university studies. I was visiting her with my parents for the traditional Saturday evening reception. My father told my grandmother: "Julius will come again to visit you to get your blessing." In the afternoon, the old grandmother gave me her blessing in accordance with the old tradition by putting her hands on my head. While I did not understand at the time what my grandmother was saying in Hebrew, I felt nonetheless, that I was experiencing something unique.

It is typical that it was my grandmother who gave me these blessings, as in reality she was the chief of the family. Whenever there was a problem in our extended family, Grandmother considered it as her personal concern, which she tried to master in her own way. When she learned in some roundabout way that one of her grandchildren faced an exam, which everyone tried to keep from her, she created a fasting day. Similarly, when she believed that my father, while carrying out some business obligation, would be arriving at home after the beginning of the Sabbath, she took this sin upon herself. She then tried to compensate for his misdeed by fasting. I remember my old grandmother only in the same mood of joy and happiness.

My grandfather reached the age of 103 years. He was already over ninety years old when he complained to me that "the boys" (as he referred to my rather dignified father and his brothers) had sent a medical doctor to visit him. He did not need a physician and never had. He must have been a man who possessed a solid body.

My father told me that some other family's money originated from 15 Talers that my grandparents had given to them, but not by choice. The head of that other family was a carrier of loads, who was noted for having a loose mouth, as is not uncommon among carriers both within and outside Jewish circles. In response to some unbecoming comments, Grandfather gave him a solid beating. Thereupon, the man went to bed and claimed to have suffered serious damage. My grandmother corrected this damage by giving the victim 15 Talers, which apparently brought about the victim's speedy recovery. Even allowing for all exaggerations, the beating must have been rather solid.

My grandfather's greatest pleasure was to sit in my father's business. Rather early in the day, while Father was at the market, my grandfather would appear in the office and ask the employees confidentially: "Is the old man already here?" As long as the reply was negative, he went into conversation with the employees. In the course of each morning, many acquaintances of Grandfather came to the office to transact some business. They all carried on some small talk with the old man. Grandfather's stay in the office also had some rewards. Not only wheat for the feeding of chickens, but also alcoholic beverages were available in the business for resale. With time, a custom developed that when a distiller delivered some spirits, Grandfather received a bottle, as a sample. These samples came originally in small bottles but eventually the size of the sample bottles grew until it was rather amazing to see the volume of these samples.

Although Grandfather adhered to all traditional customs, he was rather critical in his religious outlook. Whereas my parents and we, their children, belonged to the Liberal Brothers Congregation, my grandparents belonged to the so-called Old Synagogue, in the *Judenstrasse* ["*Jewish Street*"]. By the way, my father was among the founders of the local "Reform Congregation," where, as early as the middle of the nineteenth century, organ music was already incorporated in the service. As my father, who was on the board of directors of the community and even served for a time as its chairperson, Grandfather was treated with full respect in the Old Synagogue. Even after he reached the age of ninety, my grandfather was given the honor of saying the *Maphtir* prayer on Yom Kippur.

Yom Kippur left me with many memories of the grandparents. It was understood that both grandparents fasted on that day. In spite of the objections of his physicians, Grandfather fasted, even when he was already nearly one hundred years old. Only after my grandmother died, did Grandfather have the courage to accept a modified version of the doctor's advice and drink a cup of coffee during that day. We assembled at the Brothers' Congregation for Yom Kippur prayers by standing or sitting near my father's corner seat. We organized a schedule so that almost every hour someone went over to the other congregation to see how our grandfather was faring. As most people who attended the Old Synagogue, Grandfather wore a traditional robe with a white silken *kippa* [*yarmulke*] and over it a fur hat. Picking up Grandfather from the Old Synagogue was considered to be the highest honor. This honor was seldom granted to me, as my elder siblings asked for it. We did not argue much with them, as we were rather hungry by that time. I do remember, however, the deep impression that was imprinted in me when at the end of the service Rabbi Feilchenfeld exclaimed, *"Adonai hu ha elohim"* [*"Adonai is the Lord"*]. When the whole congregation responded in unison to this prayer, one could not help but have that imprinted in one at the end of the service.

Following the end of Yom Kippur, we raced home to drink a cup of coffee. This was followed at once by many sweet cakes, which usually resulted in a need by all members of the family to consume major quantities of sodium bicarbonate. Next, the whole family moved to the grandparents' house. Our grandfather welcomed us calmly, but Grandmother's face lit up, as someone who was granted a special favor.

I was born in the part of Posen known as the Old Town on Grossen Gerberstrasse, in the house of Mrs. Jenny Stranz. I remember about this rather talkative lady an event that signified the awakening of energy in my young person. Within our family I was generally addressed as "Juschu," which is a Polish abbreviation of my name. From a visit to a resort, Mrs. Stranz brought a cup with the inscription in Polish: "For dear Juzu." In our family only my father spoke Polish. While the rest of us did not know even one word of that language, Father was reputed to have spoken excellent Polish. This inscription on the cup convinced my spiteful brothers that I should be called Juzu. This resulted in lively fights and most serious warnings to all those who would call me Juzu. Only thanks to my mother's intervention, I did not have to carry out my threats. Apparently, the fact that I had a Polish wet nurse resulted in this name. This also caused me to speak Polish before I learned to speak German. With the departure of the wet nurse, my language skills also disappeared. When I was seven years old, we moved to Breitenstrasse. This was a major event, as the new apartment had an entrance hall with three windows, which impressed the whole family. The house belonged to a Christian family by the name of Werner, with whom we got along harmoniously. Breitenstrasse was also in the Old Town section.

Only later, when I was already a student, our family moved to Wilhelmsplatz in the New Town. There we lived in a very presentable but rather impractical apartment. Only after that move were the locations of the business and the apartment finally separated. My parents lived in that house in the Berlinerstrasse next to the Wilhelmplatz until their death.

I started attending the Friedrich Wilhelm Gymnasium [*German high schools are called "gymnasiums"*] from the ninth grade. A teacher by the name of Geisler prepared me for the ninth grade. This tutoring was needed because, at the age of six, I had to undergo an operation on my left hand. I could, therefore, not start my studies at the high school at the proper time. I had to be operated on by a famous surgeon by the name of Langenbeck [*likely Bernhard von Lagenbeck, a well-known surgeon credited with pioneering the idea of a surgical residency*] who tried, with limited success, to remove what is known as "Swimmer's Skin Formation" in my left hand [*this condition appears to have been webbed fingers*]. I still remember vividly the persona of both Langenbeck and his assistant, who, I believe, was named Professor Koenig. My father did not want to take me to a hospital. I was therefore brought to be operated on in a kosher hotel that was named, in a characteristic fashion, "King of Portugal," on Koenigstrasse in Berlin.

The operation would be scorned by today's standards. At that time they did not know how to prevent the reunification of the separated skin. Several days after the operation the stitches had to be removed, as I was suffering from severe pain. They put the cover of a cigar box under the hand in order to spread the skin. I had to live for several days with this wooden board. Nonetheless, I did not become infected. Never in my life will I forget the impression made on me by the application of chloroform, which was applied during the operation. I can still feel, as I did then, when the cloth with chloroform was put on me and how I felt that everything was coming to an end. The impression left on me by this sudden end was so strong that I still believe that death will not bring me any surprises.

These events in Berlin were, of course, among my most vivid memories of early childhood. Actually, I do remember only a few events from these early years. One was at the time when Uncle Isidor Brodnitz returned from Chile. I was at that time two or three years old. I would probably not have remembered that event but for a mishap that took place at that time. My brother Martin, who was about one year younger than me, had an accident that did not exactly improve the appearance of his white outfit.

The other early event that I remember was the homecoming of the soldiers in the year 1871. I was then almost five years old. My father owned a house on what was then called Mullen Street, which was subsequently renamed Viktoria Street. An officer, who served in the army during the war, lived on the lowest floor of the building. We watched the parade from the window of this apartment. I do not remember many details about that day. I do remember, however, that we threw flowers out of the window and that I was impressed by the fact that my older brothers were allowed to form part of an honor lane, at the entrance gate to the town.

I remember also the enormous impression that the Palace in Berlin made on me. The impression was such that when I visited Berlin again in the sixth grade of grammar school, I was able to find the way from Koenig Street to the Palace.

Another lasting impression was left with me when, at the chapel of the Palace, I saw the young prince, who was to become Wilhelm II [*Wilhelm II ruled Germany from 1888 to 1918; he was a major cause of World War I (1914–1918) and abdicated after Germany lost the war. He died in exile in the Netherlands in 1941*]. He was about ten years old at that time and was wearing the uniform of an Officer of the Guard and was decorated with a big, decorative, star-shaped medal.

Finally, I remember a visit to Circus Renz. I was very frightened and had to leave the arena. When I returned to take my place, I found that a clown had taken my seat.

I passed through secondary school with some difficulties. I had a problem in the last half-year before starting the Latin high school. The teacher of that grade was an older man by the name of Friedrich. We all had a jolly time in that class, with the result that about three-fourths of the class had to repeat that grade. Actually, I do not remember that having to repeat the grade was of much concern to me. Within me, however, this experience must have had some effect, as, from that grade onward I was always ranked either second or first in my class. Almost throughout most of my schooldays, Richard Samter sat next to me in the first or second seat. He was the highly talented son of a physician from Posen. Richard had the bad luck of having become almost blind while studying law. With much drive he succeeded to work for a while as a lawyer but with time, he was forced to stop working without having earned a pension.

Our high school followed the old traditions and emphasized only the humanities. It was rather dull. Of all the teachers at the high school, I can only remember one-and-a-half teachers who were really educators. Senior Teacher Hubert, who, I believe, was in charge of the ninth and tenth grades, understood how to add to the subject-matter knowledge based on his life's experience. The so-called half teacher was Director Noetel who supervised my senior studies and who had an understanding of language that bordered on poetry.

It was a real pleasure to listen to him read Homer or Horace. This talent was, however, negated by his inability to communicate with young people. I got along with him very well, and he was very helpful to me, even before I took my final exams. He expected all students to be able to translate Homer and Horace in the manner that he had taught it. That was, of course, an impossibility. The students set up a well-organized information service. Each student wrote the translation of one section of Homer or Horace. In this manner, each of the students obtained an excellent translation. Noetel lectured the whole hour long without having to look at the text, as he had fully memorized it.

As luck would have it, shortly before the final exam, he requested both my Horace and Homer texts in order to check some points. He was shocked to note that the whole copy was already translated. I thought that this would result in a death sentence for me, especially since I had missed the first quarter of the school year because of a gastric infection. As a result of having missed so much of that semester, I was convinced that I had not made up the missed studies and was dependent on the good will of my teacher. Noetel never mentioned this event. In fact, he requested that I be excused from the verbal final exam, which was rather uncommon in those days. Following my graduation I thanked

Noetel from the bottom of my heart. I do hope that these thanks may also have helped future students.

As I think back about the long time that I spent at the high school, I can only repeat what I said at the anniversary of our school to the old teachers who were still there: "I experienced a fair amount of monotony in the high school. I had seen enough stupidity among the teachers and the students. However, I never experienced meanness among either teachers or students." Good spirit controlled all our relationships. There were a significant number of Jews in our high school. I attended the school during the period of Stoecker/Treitscke [*see previous explanation on page 79*]. Nonetheless, neither the teachers nor the fellow students had ever behaved in an anti-Semitic moblike fashion or in any other form of anti-Semitism. Although I have been complaining since my youth about injustice done to me or to others, these were only cases of stupidity. I can only recall one such case.

When I was in the fifth grade, that is, in the tenth year of my life, the two leading students in each class were given the responsibility to supervise the class during recess. As such, they had the right to report to the teacher those students who were disruptive during recess. This was done by writing the names of the offenders on the blackboard in the classroom. When someone was reported three times, he was given a bad mark on his report card. On a given day, my friend, who was one of the supervisors, was absent from school. A student approached the teacher of our class, I believe that his name was Senior Teacher Schieche, and asked whether he could replace the missing supervisor. The teacher consented to have this student as supervisor for the day. The result of this decision was that this student wrote on the blackboard the names of all the students in the class as having misbehaved during the recess. I felt obliged to tell this student: "Just because you have been named supervisor for a day is not a reason for you to report the whole class."

The student complained to the teacher, and the teacher proceeded by noting in the class record: "Brodnitz tried to prevent an official from fulfilling his duty."

It was the custom in our school that a black mark that was not repeated would be crossed out at the end of the quarter. I recall vividly how I had to overcome serious hesitations before I went to Teacher Schieche and tried to point out that this was the only black mark on my record and that it could, therefore, be left off my report card. Scheiche retorted by telling me solemnly that what I had done was so serious that the note of censure could not be erased. Even now I still remember the feeling of disdain with which I looked down upon this teacher.

In general, however, I can only remember the good spirit of the Friedrich Wilhelm Gymnasium. After all, it was the product of traditions put in place by directors such as Schaper, Schwartz, and Noetel. During my days, the students were well integrated, regardless of their religious beliefs. Not only did we not say bad things about others, but also, to a large extent, we started relationships that lasted throughout our whole lives.

There grew a wish among those who went to school with me to form in Berlin an association by the name *Guarthonia* [*the origin of this name is unclear*], which I also joined when I came to Berlin for the fourth semester of university. Among those of my generation who belonged to this association were Siegfried Brodnitz, Fritz Orgler, Karl Kielhorn, and Felix Kaempfer. I remember with special fondness Richard Matzel, who was a fellow student and belonged to our organization until he passed the national tests and decided to become a member of the Catholic clergy. Even after he became a member of the clergy, he knew how to maintain his old relationships. I was very pleased that, when he was hospitalized as the result of a serious illness, he requested that I come once more to visit him. I was an attorney at that time, living in Berlin. I traveled at once to Posen. He was already lying in the so-called morphine room, but he recognized me at once and forgot in an instant his clerical life, instead reminiscing about our days as students. He then lost consciousness, and within a few hours he died.

Selecting a profession was a bit strange for me. Considering that a strong liberal arts environment dominated my high school, I had become full of knowledge by the time I reached the upper grades. At times, during the summer, I would get up at three in the morning in order to read classic Greek and Latin texts. In those days school began at seven o'clock.

I wavered between the idea of becoming a liberal clergyman and studying the old Egyptian language or the study of classical Greek and Latin. I liked this idea very much. I only gave up this concept because my father pointed out to me with great urgency that the odds were very slim that a Jew would get a teaching position in linguistics. He felt that my chances as a Jew to get further than teaching in a high school were very remote. Moreover, even a career as a teacher of languages appeared to me to be rather unlikely, which caused me to give up the study of education.

This led to a serious wavering on my part, and I told my father that I had decided not to study but take up business instead. Father clearly knew me better than I had known myself. I don't mean to say that I would have become a poor businessman. This in turn led to future developments, which one could not have anticipated at that time. Father recognized that I would find satisfaction only by following an academic career. I attended the university in Leipzig because Father felt that I had worked so hard to graduate from high school that he wanted me to take the time to have a merry life as a student.

In Leipzig I attended the classes of the well-known romantic studies teacher named Windscheid [*perhaps Bernhard Windschied, one of the fathers of the German Civil Code*].

It was thanks to him that I became a lawyer. I had assumed that law consisted only of putting paragraphs together. Windscheid in Leipzig showed me that law also consisted of the development of concepts and ideas as part of the legal work. Through his influence, I became an enthusiastic lawyer. I believe that if I had to select my profession again, I would have selected the same profession. In particular, I would have selected to become active as a free representative [rather than as an employee of the government or a big company].

I spent two semesters at the university in Leipzig, although actually most of my second semester was dedicated mainly to the study of dancing in the great ballroom and to riding trains. The only teacher at the university whom I found impressive, in addition to Windscheid, was the economics professor Roscher [perhaps Wilhelm Georg Friedrich Roscher].

As I recall the period I spent in Leipzig, I remember that it contributed much to my musical education. Unfortunately, I was completely uneducated in the arts of music. Because of my problem with my left hand, it was assumed that I would have been incapable of performing music. This was certainly a mistake. I could have found a way to practice playing music, even if only with one hand.

Music, therefore, became an unhappy love, which I had spent many hours in my youth missing. Yet, unhappy love runs deepest. This may have led to the development of an understanding of music uncommon amongst amateurs. In Leipzig I was exposed for the first time to the wonderful symphonies. Old Master Reinecke was the director of the so-called Gewandhaus [perhaps composer and educator Carl Reinecke].

A rehearsal of the orchestra under the leadership of old Reinecke would take up the whole morning. Initially, the whole symphony was played from beginning to end. Then he reviewed each segment with the orchestra, and then the orchestra repeated each section. One could clearly sense how the conductor influenced the performance of an orchestra.

At that time, the orchestra in Leipzig was very set on the music of the old school. I recall that Reinecke was very courageous by conducting for a whole week only compositions by the then-new [*Johannes*] Brahms. A well-respected musical writer said about the Brahms Lieder that they were actually not songs. A musical newspaper wrote at that time that they could not understand how Reinecke expected a noted violinist such as the Leipzig orchestra's [*Adolph*] Brodsky to play Brahms' Violin Concerto.

Even disregarding the Gewandhaus, life in Leipzig was very exciting. For 90 Pfennig, we were able to get wonderful seats in the last rows of the orchestra. A copious selection of programs was performed at the opera. One could hear operas that are seldom performed elsewhere. That was during the period in which Stegemann had the unusual luck to discover and secure the services of some outstanding performers for the Leipzig Opera House.

Berlin, June 30, 1926

As I recall these memories haphazardly, I would like to fill in some points that I missed.

My early school years were during a period of much excitement. A cultural war was going on between the German and Polish students. Our school, the Friedrich Wilhelm Gymnasium, was a German school. Next to our school was the Marien High School, which was mainly attended by Polish students. Whereas our high school was Evangelist, the Marien High School was Catholic, as at that time in Posen, being Polish and Catholic were virtually identical. This led to almost daily fights between the students of the two schools. We selected a leader of our armed forces whom we followed. We all had at least one fighter among us. When I was in the eighth or ninth grade, I carried a sharpened block of wood with me. I cannot recall ever having made use of this weapon. One was, however, always prepared to be attacked. I do recall that one of us was buried in the snow by the Polish kids and was left there for a while. I do not believe that anyone was ever seriously injured in these attacks.

Director Schwarz was an ardent nationalist who cared about honor. Whenever he sat in the garden of his home, he was attacked by thrown stones. Director Schwarz was a most interesting person. He was one of the first to study the prehistoric period of Posen. He was able to generate remarkable interest in this topic. His greatest pleasure was to take the students of the upper grades for an outing. Each of the students was equipped with a small shovel, and we searched prehistoric sites. From these digs he, had accumulated a significant collection of urns. During these excavations I also saw for the first time parts of the remains of ancient mammoths. He was a very modest man. Typically, for as long as I had known him, he and his many sons always wore outfits made from the same fabric, which Director Schwarz had purchased in one big lot. He had an understanding for the weakness of his students. One always had the feeling that one was dealing with a person who had developed fatherly feelings in the course of bringing up his own children. He also used these skills when dealing with his students.

As I mentioned before, the number of real educators among the teachers in our high school was very limited. There were in the school some interesting personalities, one of whom was Professor Starke. He had a real temper, which he also demonstrated at the beer bar. I was in the same grade as his son, Paul Starke, during almost all my school days. Thanks to that, and to the intercession of Mother Starke, my classmates enjoyed occasional forbearance. Occasionally, through the action of Mother Starke, we were allowed to rewrite assignments in [*Professor Starke's*] history class. When this occurred, the teacher complained that the devil would catch us if we ever try to hide again behind his wife.

We also had some interesting math personalities in our school. Although I had not had the opportunity to study with Professor Neydeker, he was considered one of Posen's personalities. When our school celebrated its fiftieth anniversary, Headmaster von Guentner, himself a long-time Posen resident, made a nice speech. Among other things, he said that he actually did not live up to the expectations of his teacher, Mr. Neydeker, who had predicted that he would end up on the gallows.

Predictions of teachers are always most peculiar. For example, the classes of Professor Pohl were always highly amusing. This teacher had already had many years of service. In his class was a student who was a member of a large family from Koenigsberg, whose older brother, a former student of Pohl, was already a famous mathematician in Heidelberg. When he reproached the younger brother, he said: "You are a damn fool," but at once he corrected himself saying, "I'd better be careful, as I already said the same to your famous brother."

A Professor Kretschmer [*who followed Neydecker*] unfortunately suffered from serious neurological problems and enjoyed with a passion when he could confront students. This, of course made him completely unsuited to be a teacher at a school. I attended only a few classes with him. I do recall, however, stories by fellow students about his classes. His replacement, with whom I studied math and natural science in the upper grades, was an incompetent by the name of Professor von Schaeven. He was especially incapable of developing any interest in natural science among his students. Learning by rote was practiced. I recall that we studied optics with him for a whole semester. Whenever one was asked by the teacher to solve a problem one could, almost in one's sleep, reply by saying $1/a \times 1/b = 1/f$. I have to admit that, even today, I don't know the true meaning of this formula, which I had often recited.

This teacher was, however, very typical of the thought process customary in those days at the high school. One thing that I heard from this teacher stayed with me and gave me some lasting value. I was not an outstanding mathematician. Yet one day I was able to solve a difficult mathematical equation. The teacher exclaimed: "You have found a Truth. When one thinks or works with science, one must be satisfied and consider oneself lucky when one discovers a Truth, even when the utility of this Truth is not obvious at once. No Truth disappears without leaving some sort of a trail." These were probably not the exact words used by this humorless teacher, but this was the spirit of what he said. Perhaps because he said it in a clumsy and dry way, this saying left a strong and lasting impression on me.

The physical exercise classes in our high school were not much better than the studies of natural sciences. Professor Schmidt, who was promoted from teaching in an elementary school, caused the PE class to be considered by nine of ten of the students an "hour of suffering." Our skills in PE were minimal. The "heroes" of our classes were primarily students who had to repeat several grades and who were, therefore, older and who towered over the rest of us in both size and power.

This teacher was also our singing coach. One must admit that he was able to make us achieve significant accomplishments in this subject. In the winter, at the midpoint of our singing lessons, we were asked to perform at local hospitals. These concerts were accompanied also by the performance of some short acts. The director of these performances was an art teacher by the name of Wagner, who was unequaled in his skills as a teacher. He started our art lessons by having us draw perfect vertical lines without the aid of tools [*freehand*]. Many of my classmates did not progress past this first subject. From the eighth grade on, art classes were optional. I did not participate in the theatrical programs. The reason for this was that by the time I reached the upper grade, from which most participants were selected, the school had eliminated this program. The performances during those days were of *Wallenstein, Tasso*, etc. Nowadays, the way our teacher directed these shows would be considered overly modern. He was an absolute admirer of the right-wing [*political*] movements. Enthusiasm replaced practice and physical appearance. I recall, for example, a performance of *Tasso* [*the legend of Tasso's doomed love made him a romantic hero to Byron and Goethe*] in which a capable and enthusiastic fellow student by the name of Muetzel performed the main role. He was a most capable student but was not exactly suited for this role as one of his legs was shorter than the other. This outstanding student was the son of a respected lawyer in Posen. He represented for me the danger in being an outstanding student. He became a real pain at the university and was always in danger of being drunk. I lost contact with him in later days.

The oldest teacher at the high school was Professor Moritz. He taught Homer and Plato to the whole generation. He was a fossilized type of teacher who was able to claim that, in writing *Apologia,* Plato's most significant accomplishment was that he placed four conjunctions in a row, something that no other Greek writer of his era was able to do.

When I returned to my high school for the celebration of the school's seventy-fifth anniversary, I found that only a few of my old teachers were still there. Professor Rummler, who taught us German, has been promoted to Master Teacher. He was a lively gentleman, and I have often thought about words that he taught me. Thanks to his admonitions, I also stopped misusing certain words. For example, when I wrote in a sentence, "The Roman was driven to a peak," Professor Rummler stopped me and said, "Imagine the Roman who was driven to the peak." This remark has led me in later writing and reviewing some of my speeches to remember the "Roman driven to the peak" and thereby to have saved myself from some sorry expressions.

Our family was well represented at the Friedrich Wilhelm Gymnasium. All my brothers attended this school. At one time, we had in one classroom three with the name "Brodnitz" and one with the family name "von Brodnitzki." The three with the Brodnitz name were my cousin Siegfried, my brother Martin, and me. This, however, lasted only for a short time. Students who were part of the Easter Quarter and the Fall Quarter grades were in one classroom. As a result of the high school being overfilled, students who belonged to four subgroups were put together in one room. The same studies were taught twice each year. As a result of this rushed coverage of the material, students were only rarely able to earn a "Satisfactory" grade in these classes [*often leading to students having to repeat grades*]. My brother Martin was a very bright young man who was not very interested in his studies. This led to a constant enmity between him and his teachers. He developed a good sense of humor. He had to repeat several grades and graduated a few semesters after me.

He had Professor Moritz as a teacher in some of the lower grades. This teacher was in the habit of correcting students' papers with great care. This teacher used a special set of markings to point out mistakes in students' work. For example, he would cross out certain mistakes, use small stars for others, and snake markings for others. One day Professor Moritz told me that he felt very sorry for my father, whom he had known and appreciated. In answer to my surprised reaction, the teacher explained that he thought that my brother had lost his mind. In one of these papers, my brother was told that his work was very bad and included twelve "snakes," to which Martin retorted that the local zoo would be happy to hear that, as he [*Martin*] intended to donate these snakes to the zoo. Professor Moritz exclaimed: "The poor boy has lost his mind."

Siegfried Brodnitz and I not only went through school together, we also did our university studies together. Both as students and later in life, we were, without doubt, completely different people. Nonetheless, we had spent our life together, as few friends do. This was the case because we respected each other's personality and allowed each other to be what we wanted to be. This was not easy, especially during our university days. Even when we appeared to drift apart, we always found each other again.

During my school days, I also visited Berlin. As a reward for earning a promotion to the twelfth grade, I traveled with my brother Martin to visit our sister Fanny. Fanny, with her newlywed husband, Oskar Lipschitz, took us around Berlin.

We were able to pack a lot into the two weeks that we stayed in Berlin. At the opera, we were able to enjoy a performance of *Troubadour*, with the great Marianne Brandt. At the main serious theater of that time, we saw *Der Stoerenfried* by [Roderich] Benedix, in which Berndal, Döring, and Frieb-Blumauer were acting. During the Easter holidays, we were able to go to the great theatric event when *Wohltaetigen Frauen* was performed at the Wallner Theater. At that performance, all the stars of the day were involved, including the comic Enlels: she played the role of Lohndiener Pfeffermann, who exclaimed the now famous saying: "I had seen the balance in your savings account, and that is enough for me."

We were seated in the upper level of the theater while Oskar and Fanny had seats in the orchestra section of the theater. After the show, my sister told me she saw that I was standing for much of the show shaking with laughter. She was afraid I would laugh so hard that I would lose my balance and fall to the lower level of the theater. This skill of hearty laughter I have fortunately not lost in my later years.

During the time of my studies in Leipzig, I had taken my first trip to the mountains. Aided by a small contribution, I traveled to Saxon Switzerland [*a district in Germany*] via Dresden. In Dresden I met with Siegfried, who at that time was studying in Berlin. Those were great days. We stayed on the trip until we had just enough money left to return to our universities. I had only 60

Pfennig left when I arrived back in Leipzig, and with this I had to cover the cost of my supper. Fortunately, on the following morning the mailman brought me my next allowance. This was the normal situation with me. Seldom was I able to pay the postman his due or give him a tip. Normally, I told him to withhold both from the balance that was due to me. I remember vividly how, standing in front of the Panorama Restaurant, which in those days I regarded as rather good, I had reached into my pocket to count the change to see whether or not I still had the required 60 Pfennig. As I was reaching for my change, I dropped the money. I must have been a very sad sight, as people all around me picked up the change and handed it to me. At the end, I was still left with 40 Pfennig, and I could order some cheese and a glass of beer.

Economically, we lived in those days as rather well-off students. With a monthly allowance of 120 Marks, I was considered rather rich. I do recall how in Leipzig I found myself four days before the end of the month with only 1.5 Marks. I had prepaid for my lunch meals, and a package from home provided for the dinners. With only 1.5 Marks, I could not risk going to my customary beer hall and possibly spending the total amount in one evening. Instead, I went for three evenings to the Old Town Theater in Leipzig, where for 30 Pfennig per evening I was able to see shows that were not of recent vintage. I ended the three nights with 60 Pfennig in my pocket.

Teresina Tua, a pretty Italian violinist, was rather famous in those days. For 50 Pfennig, we could get a good student's ticket to her performance. Following her performance, after listening to this talented, young, and pretty performer, we stood next to the horses of her carriage. She handed us each a rose from the bouquets that were given to her at the end of the performance. Consequently, I returned to my room on the last day of the month with a rose from Teresina and the princely treasure of 10 Pfennig.

For our third semester, I transferred from Leipzig to the university in Freiburg. Fritz Orgler, Karl Kielhorn, and Siegfried Brodnitz joined me in this move to the south. The months that I spent in Freiburg were wonderful. In our circle of friends, we found a group with similar interests. I have lost contact with many of them. There was a law student by the name of Keller, who was the son of a state judge in Colmar. In spite of his young age, this man suffered from diabetes, which did not prevent him from partaking in many of our hikes.

I also recall a fellow student who came from an aristocratic family by the name of von Foerster, who originated in Braunschweig. Together we went for hikes every Saturday evening and all of Sunday. During this semester, I learned for the first time how to enjoy nature. This caused me to transform from a person who spent his time sitting in his room to a freer-spirited student. Our trips took us to rather distant places. We regarded Basel as only a short stop from Freiburg. These trips were not expensive. Most nights were spent in guest quarters that the wine growers maintained. These quarters seldom cost us more than 50 Pfennig per night. It was wonderful to reach Saekkingen for the first time, following a hike through the Alb valley to the river Rhine!

One week there was a Catholic holiday on Thursday. We were in a seminar led by the then-young Professor Rosin, who had a good head but delivered his presentation in a boring monotone, which caused me to fall asleep. My friend Kielhorn woke me up with a note that asked me to look through the window and see how wonderful the weather was. It would be a crime not to go for a hike during the following four days. So we closed our books and left the classroom and had a war council to determine our financial condition and work on plans for the trip.

As it was shortly before the end of the month, our means were rather limited. We concluded that if we pooled our resources, it might be possible to take the trip. This was the case because one of us had received his monthly allowance ahead of time. We left on our way and were singing as we reached the Rhine and then proceeded to walk to Schaffhausen, where thanks to wonderful weather, I saw for the first time the shining, silvery Alps reflected against the sky. We kept worrying all along that some unexpected expense would prevent us from paying for our return trip. One of us had the responsibility to find in each village a place where one could sleep at a low-budget price. All the hotels at which a porter welcomed one were eliminated from consideration.

In Freiburg, I got to know a completely different interpretation of Catholic belief than the one I was used to from my experience with those of Polish background. In Posen, the feast of Corpus Christi was observed with gloomy fatalism. Here, on the other hand, I saw for the first time how young women and youngsters spent a nice summer day celebrating the Holy One with music and showing naive joy in the beautiful world.

My brother Alfons picked me up at the end of the semester for a trip to Switzerland. Siegfried and I had previously tried to visit Switzerland during Pentecost. Unfortunately, it rained so much on that occasion we were in danger of using up our small travel allowance without getting to see the country. We therefore decided to return home using the shortest route.

The Swiss trip turned out to be a wonderful time. We undertook strenuous hikes, and we admired the majestic mountains. It was perhaps to be expected that on our return trip to our home, we ridiculed the mountains of our country. The correct attitude to the country's landscape is hard to appreciate as a youngster. As one gets older, one develops a deeper appreciation of the scenery. When I returned to Switzerland as a young lawyer and visited with my dear friends who were staying in Eisenach, I no longer suffered from this opinion but enjoyed our German mid-level mountains. By now, the high mountains were no longer a novelty for me. Even in those mountains, one cannot solve all human problems. These are observations that are hard to comprehend as a youngster. From Switzerland, I traveled down the Rhine to Mainz. At that time I came to Köln for my first visit.

The rest of my studies were spent in Berlin. A nice circle of old friends from *"Guarthonia"* days in Posen gathered there at that time. We lived as beer-loving students but also studied with enthusiasm.

I received motherly love at the home of my sister Fanny and my brother-in-law Oskar Lipschitz. Fanny Lipschitz, with whom I was very close until her early end, was an unusual woman who possessed all the nice personality traits of my mother. She experienced the sorrows of life in all their fullness. Our parents' love spoiled her without making her immodest. Her husband honored her, and she, who was clever enough to realize that her appearance was not very pretty, appreciated his knightly manner. (Her face was partially pockmarked, and her pretty neck was rather disfigured by goiter). She was very motherly by nature, and she was bitterly disappointed that she was left childless.

Fanny was also smart enough to see the difference between the successful way business was run at her father's house and the way her husband carried it out. She must have suffered when her husband gave up his small leather-goods business and instead dedicated his efforts to speculating with their funds on the stock market, which led, within a short time, to the loss of their funds. Nonetheless, I never heard from this woman a word or even a hint of anger at her husband for his failure. With much love, she dedicated herself to her siblings and their children so that she acted as their grandmother in the fullest sense of the word. Although she was an aunt to those children, she behaved and felt like their grandmother.

I'll never forget my last visit to her. She was in bed with an inflammation of her lungs. Surprisingly, less than two years earlier, her husband died of a similar infection. She was aware that she was seriously ill, and I felt that the end was near. She was always very interested in my professional and family activities. But as I was turning to leave, she called out loving words, and I felt that these were the words of someone who had already left this world. As I closed the door of her room, I quietly said to myself, *"Les adieux."* Such a farewell and love were clearly her way of saying goodbye, in spite of the fact that her sickness did not appear to be at a critical stage at that moment. Unfortunately, by the following night I was summoned to her deathbed.

Berlin, July 1, 1926

My studies in Berlin came to an end when I took the State Examination for Candidates for Higher Civil Service Positions [*"Refrendarexamen" in German*] at the Law Chambers. As I have habitually done, I took the hard way in taking this exam. While I am generally a quick decision maker, I have always had a difficult time putting my answers on paper in a written exam. Undoubtedly, I suffered from an exaggerated sense of responsibility. Wistfully and with a heavy heart, I said goodbye to the university and to my overgrown fellow students, who had now all become Philistines [*that is, common people, nonintellectuals*].

I had to spend my period as a legal trainee at the regional higher court for the district of Posen. The president of this court was at that time a Mr. Franz. This man was the brother of the well-known actress named Ellen Franz-Meiningen, the wife of the Grand Herzog von Meiningen [*that was one of his titles, not his name; his full title was Duke Georg II of Saxe-Meiningen*].

This judge, who originated from Düsseldorf, was preceded by a bad reputation. When a show by the name *"Rauber"* [*"Robbers"*] was presented in Düsseldorf and included the words, "Franz was the name of the scoundrel," the audience broke out in frenzied cheering and all looked in the direction of the court president.

He belonged to those who claimed heatedly that they were not anti-Semites but who, by their actions, did everything to make life difficult for Jews. Although Mr. Franz was a converted Jew, he performed this dirty work as the Chief Justice. He tried to block entrance to official positions by all Jewish candidates by requiring them to show that they possessed excessive sources of income. These demands were only made of Jewish candidates. The prevailing rule at that time was that during the first nine months of training, a candidate had to appear in courts in which no more than three judges were sitting on each case. So I had the luck to be sent to the very Polish town of Nest Koschmin [*probably Kozmin, 74 km south-southeast of Posen*]. This was a place where the words of the Baron von Gaudy apply, "Man and Beast eat from the same trough."

One may think that transferring from Berlin to a place such as this would be hard to take for a young man. However, such was not my case. I did, however, retire quickly from where, while eating, I was served at a table reserved for honored guests. I learned at that time to retire to my own modest four walls and found my satisfaction in reading. During the balance of my practical training period, I also spent time in Schneidemuehl [*Pila, 83 km north of Posen*] and in Gnesen [*a location in the district of Bromberg*]. I am thankful for what these periods have given me. I have had plenty of opportunities for reflection during my years as a high school and university student. In these small towns, I learned to make these interests a basis for the rest of my life.

As I traveled from place to place, I carried with me a box filled with many books. When I unpacked these books in my new abode, I felt at home in the new place. By the way, I can add that when one keeps one's eyes open, one can get to know in a small town a large number of unique individuals. If one only tries, one can dedicate one's time to one's interests in a way that is not possible when living in a big city.

In each town in which I found myself as a trainee, I developed good friends. From my stay in Gnesen I remember especially a simple man who had an unusual desire to learn. This man was an auctioneer by trade. His name was Fromm. This man was very enthusiastic without necessarily being critical in his evaluations. With his modest means, he built up a significant library. He also owned a wonderful collection of copper engravings. I spent many evenings enjoying his collection.

During the time I was in Koschmin, my eldest brother, Hugo, got engaged. I traveled to Graetz to partake in the engagement party. This led to my first meeting with my future wife, who was twelve years old at that time. It was during that time that I also arrived at the decision to grow a beard. This decision was considered provocative by my whole family, as no one in my family had a full beard. The only exception was Uncle Isidor Brodnitz, who had returned from Chile with a beard. My decision did not stem from any awakened principles, but rather from the fact that shaving was, unfortunately, very cumbersome, and I did not trust the local barber in Koschmin, who was drunk most of the time. I had to live through a rather difficult fight with my family to avoid a forced removal of the beard.

With much happiness, we arrived at the house of the Herzfeld family in Graetz for my brother's engagement party. There we met a family with a bourgeois point of view and one that possessed a high degree of idealism and seriousness. This meeting resulted in lifelong friendship between our families.

During my training period, I traveled every weekend to Posen. From a young age, together with my brother Hugo, I became accustomed to being asked by my parents to participate in their decisions. This probably led to my being a bit more serious than my age would have suggested. I did not consider this a burden, as I believe I always had enough of a light temperament not to be oppressed by the seriousness of life.

During my period of practical training, my father's health deteriorated. This man who had been full of energy never recovered from the blow brought about by the death of my brother Felix in the year 1880.

A major portion of my training period was spent in my parents' house. It was not easy for me to travel to Berlin for the exam that was taken by civil servants who had completed their trainee period. I did so with the knowledge that this way would not lead me back to my hometown. My father suffered very much because of the progression of the so-called Parkinson's disease. Only the painful way in which my father held himself made it possible for him to maintain a correct appearance, in spite of the sickness.

Following my exam, I had a conversation with Mr. Franz, who was president of the court, which convinced me to give up any thought of a career in civil service or in the courts. I came to the president of the court after passing the exam to inquire about a position as a court official in the district of Posen. He received me in a friendly manner but proceeded to tell me that he felt obliged to inform me that as a Jew, I had only limited chances for advancement in the courts. I told him that as a legal trainee, I had developed great respect for attested rights and believed that judges would not consider facts other than the honesty of people who came before them and their obedience to their duties. I regrettably saw that my point of view required serious reconsideration if I were to gather the courage and pursue a legal career. Franz replied that, for heaven's sake, he did not intend to drive me away from pursuing a career as a judge. It was indeed possible that a Jew could advance as a judge. In fact, it did occur that when Christian colleagues and other important people reported good observations about a Jewish judge, he gladly suggested that person for promotion. I responded that during my years of studies, I never pursued those people who ran to my boss to tell him whether or not I was a decent person and fulfilled my obligations. As a consequence of this meeting, the following day I handed in my resignation. This was not very easy for me. I, and those around me too, were of the opinion that my true calling was becoming a lawyer. On contemplating it, I thought that this, rather than a career in the courts, was more suited to my nature [*in other words, he decided on a career as a lawyer in private practice rather than as a judge or civil servant*].

Early on, when I became a lawyer, I considered the possibility that this was to become just a station in my life's passage. I soon set aside this point of view, as I found pleasure in the profession and in helping others manage their lives, which is the job of an attorney who acts in compassion. If I had to face the decision again today, I would not select any other occupation.

Early in my career as a lawyer, serious illness took first my mother and then my father. In my first year as an attorney, my mother was on her way back from Karlsbad and was planning to go with me to visit my sister Selma, who had recently gotten married and lived in Danzig. I was one of the first to discover that my mother had died.

Almost every weekend, as I went to my parents' home, and I thought about it, I always considered it a grace that I was present for the passing of this unusual woman, who passed from her life as a sacrament. My suffering father sat in the adjacent room while we were assembled around Mother's bed. I can still hear the sound of the Shma Yisrael prayer coming from the mouths of my elder brothers, which my father joined, in order to share in the last minutes of the life of his wife, with whom he was joined by unique love. It is the beauty of our Jewish life that memories of family and culture are so joined. Anyone who hears Shma Yisrael recalls memories from home, which are the root of full Jewish feeling and which are more important than all the theories one can study and learn. Following the customary manner, we left Mother's burial to the so-called *Chevra Kadisha* [*the Jewish burial society*]. The atmosphere at her deathbed was so holy that we felt that no action or word should be allowed to take away from this occasion.

In the case of Father, who followed Mother within a short time, it was unfortunately not handled in the same manner. At the insistence of his brothers, my siblings felt obligated to follow the old traditional ceremony. I was called by phone to his bedside. By the time I reached my parents' house, Father had already passed away. From his pained expression, one could see the fear that the traditional ceremony had brought to him.

Following the old Jewish tradition, my eldest brother, Hugo, took over the responsibilities of Father's role in the family. In his self-assured manner, he dispensed fatherly advice to his younger siblings, until death claimed him at the beginning of the horrible war [*World War I*].

I had very deep, friendly feelings for my brother. Not that we agreed on everything—just the opposite was often the case. Our basic points of view were rather different. But in my lifetime I had the luck to live with people who did not regard their own point of view as the only correct one. This allowed us to have a full understanding for each other even when we had differing opinions. This occurred frequently with my brother Hugo, who was much older than I [*Hugo was born in 1854; Julius in 1866*]. The same was true for his wife, with whom I was very close ever since she joined our family. I am especially thankful to the tolerance of the Herzfeld parents [*the parents of Hedwig, Julius' wife, as well as the parents of the wives of Julius' brothers Hugo and Hermann*], who lived according to the strongest traditional orthodox manners, and yet accepted us with much love and tolerance from the day we first met.

From my early days as a lawyer, I recall taking up again my relations with Benno Braun, my former classmate from school. This unusually serious man left high school after he stumbled through promotion to the twelfth grade. Because of the financial conditions of his parents, he felt that he could not expect them to bear the cost of his education unless he accomplished it in the shortest time. This turned out to be fortunate for him. We had lost touch with each other. When I came to Berlin to take the State Examination for Candidates for Higher Civil Service Positions, we met again. He had taken a position in business. We have kept in close contact ever since then.

When we were both still bachelors, hardly a free day went by that we did not spend together. Through him I got closer to men of a completely different nature. The same relationship also developed with Robert Kutner, who later became a professor and who died at an early age. This firebrand and I spent wonderful hours and days together. Here too it was a sign of the solidity of our relationship that we could exchange opinions that were drastically different and yet remain very friendly.

When Robert Kutner's mother moved to Berlin after the death of her husband, she split the time between the homes of her sons. His mother became a highly appreciated motherly friend for me too, especially after the death of my mother. Then, in spite of her age, this woman was a picture to behold. With her three overly bubbly sons, she radiated with motherly care. Unfortunately, she had a series of misfortunes. Robert died young, and his wife passed away even before him. Her second son also predeceased her. I still remember her saying, "Lord, don't burden me with as much as I am able to carry." In all her suffering, this remarkable woman never lost her composure. When her eldest son left for America, after the end of the war [*World War I*], she went to bed on the day before his departure and died.

In spite of the fact that my siblings and I stayed in close contact, life became rather lonely after the death of my parents. My travels brought me frequently to Posen, where I enjoyed spending the holidays. In Posen during Whitsunday of 1898, I met little Hedwig, who in the meantime had transformed from a twelve-year-old girl to a lovely young maiden. Within a few days, I made my decision, and about that I don't have to report to my wife or to my children. Hedwig and I have built our lives as true comrades. All that I have accomplished since then is as much the result of her efforts as mine.

As I survey the past sixty years, then, I feel a deep sense of thankfulness, and the Whitsunday days of 1898 ring the loudest [*that is when he met again the young woman Hedwig had become*].

Much of my life appeared to have evolved according to some master plan. Yet, while I am not a fatalist, as I look back on my life, I have to say: "All happened as it had to be." This applies to my whole life, to my professional life and to my life outside my work. Long ago I realized that it would be a mistake to assume that I could have pursued any line of work other than law.

Because of my view of the world, I could not do anything other than serve the better part of my life working on what I believe.

As a non-observing Jew, I had to join, as a young lawyer, the *Centralverein,* the movement that was begun by Eugen Fuchs and Maximilian Horwitz. Without knowing anything about this movement, already when I lived in Koschmin as a candidate for a higher civil servant position, I put on a top hat and went to the synagogue on the Jewish holidays. I did this in order to signify my Jewish roots. I did this even though, as a student, I considered going to services a bother and tried to stay away from any religious events. It was clearly a mistake when, as a non-observant Jew, I offered my services to the Central Organization of Germans with Jewish Belief [*this is the translation of the full name of the Der Centralverein deutscher Staatsbuerger juedischen Glaubens, or C.V.*]. During the early days of my activities, I stated that I felt I could work with equal dedication and love on the concerns of any group that was denied its rights on account of its beliefs. I soon discovered that I was wrong. I soon realized that beyond being a born Jew, I felt an inner need to provide my services to the ideas of the real German Jews.

Julius and Hedwig and their sons, Fritz, Otto, and Heinz (Berlin, approximately 1915)

Similarly, I inevitably became a Freemason. From my humanistic viewpoint of the world, I had the correct feeling that my love for and involvement in Jewish subjects might cause me to lose contact with the rest of humanity [*this may be why he felt that he had to join a universal group such as the Freemasons*].

My work at the C.V. brings me in uninterrupted contact with stimulating people who enrich my life. I would like to mention just a few of them: The importance of the contributions of Maximilian Horwitz and Eugen Fuchs for us and for me has already been covered in numerous other places. With special love, I would like to mention two men who surely did not share my view of the world. These are Hirsch Hilhesheimer and Oskar Berlin, both of whom were members and leaders of *Adass Jisroel* [*a Jewish congregation in Berlin*]. It was a pleasure and stimulating for me to serve in the C.V. with members of different religious points of view. It is imperative not to forget this. Our opponents tend to ignore this. Oskar Berlin always reminds me of how the C.V. underwent substantial changes in the course of time. I recall a very thorough discussion with Oskar Berlin in which he declared, with my basic concurrence, that the difference between a German Jew and his Christian fellow citizen was only his religious belief. This was the product of the purely rational point of view that ruled the second half of the previous century [*the nineteenth century*]. It is to the credit of Eugen Fuchs that he made us aware of our inner being as German Jews. We now know that the German Jew is not the outcome of some cleverness but rather is the product of a full life.

I recall with thanks the days in which for the first time, under the flag of our organization [*the C.V.*], a so-called Jewish Day was celebrated.

Had I wanted to continue to tell this story, I would have had to write the history of the *Centralverein*. I doubt that I'll ever do that. Even these sketches would not have taken place had I not been sitting for my portrait, which was made by Professor Erich Wolfsfeld, who suggested that I use this time for gathering some memories.

Therefore, these *Memories* end with the last session with Professor Wolfsfeld.

Notes

Julius Brodnitz was born on August 19, 1866, in Schwersenz, Province of Posen, Germany, and died July 19, 1936, in Berlin, Germany.

He was the husband of Hedwig Herzfeld Brodnitz (1878–1938) and father of
- Friedrich (Fritz) Brodnitz (1899–1995)
- Otto Brodnitz (1902–1976)
- Heinz Brodnitz (1905–1984)

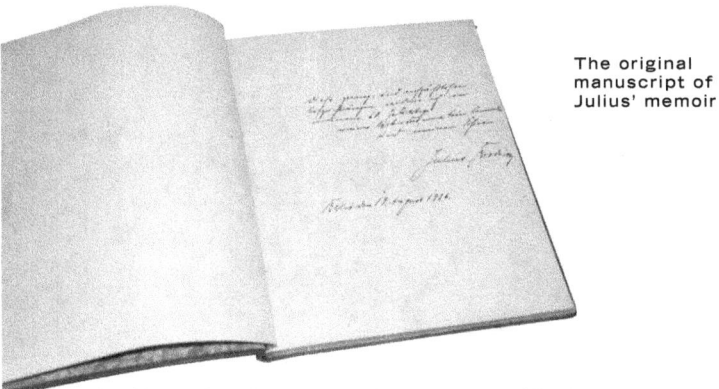

The original manuscript of Julius' memoir

Chapter 3
Hedwig Herzfeld Brodnitz

Written in 1924, with an addition made in 1931.

This picture of Hedwig Brodnitz was taken in the 1930s when these memoirs were written.

THE RECORD LEFT BEHIND by my dear mother [*Julie Badt Herzfeld*] encouraged me to put down my memories of my younger days. I do not know whether or not these notes are worthwhile, but at least the attempt has been made.

My earliest recollections deal with my first and only serious illness. I suspect these memories were, in fact, based on suggestions made by others. My dear aunt Roeschen Stern told me this story so often that I am now not sure whether or not I actually still remember the events or just their retelling. I was about two years old when my father was away on one of his frequent trips, and Mother, who was again expecting the birth of another child, had to live through the fear for my survival all alone. The cause of the concern was an infection that was called at that time the

"Sun Tan sickness," which is probably the disease known today as diphtheria.

I was supposed to undergo an operation in the throat when nature took care of events. Aunt Roeschen Stern has frequently described the event as a debt that I had owed her and for which she expected to receive my thanks. I must have been full of medications that were given to me to help fight the sickness and prevent its recurrence. This gave me resistance to all subsequent sicknesses, which, to my sorrow, prevented me from taking time off from school in all my subsequent years. I did not catch any of the normal childhood sicknesses. In spite of all my efforts, I could not catch from my younger siblings measles, mumps, etc.

I do remember, however, that after this illness I had to eat my meals alone in the children's room. I also had to wear a black band on my neck, which was treated with cinnamon. As I learned at a later date, this was recommended as a potion to which some healing qualities were ascribed. It was also decided that my throat had to be protected from any excitement, which could cause me to cry or scream. I discovered that soon enough and used it to get my way. A year later, when Hugo was born, Mother used the rare opportunity that she was bedridden to dedicate her energies to my upbringing. I was promised a piece of Grandmother's poppy cake if I vowed never to say "NO" again. There were, however, several setbacks to this vow.

The next event that left its lasting imprint on my memory was the wedding of cousin Regina Stern and Wolf Jablonski. As my wardrobe was rather limited, I was given a special dress on loan that belonged to my cousin Hella who lived in Posen. My dear aunt added, as a special favor, a light blue medallion. Both of these items gave me the feeling of being in a fairy tale, and I greatly envied their owner. The reason why Hella had much more elegant items than I had was rather simple: she was the eldest of two children, while I, as the fourth child, was not given all that much.

The wedding took place in the community's social hall. My brother Hugo wore a dress [*the custom for very young boys*] with white and black squares. I don't recall what the others wore. In any case, Hugo and I were the most important participants at that time, as far as I was concerned. My cousin Albert Stern and one of his brothers took part in the wedding party as a couple with a barrel organ, with Albert wearing one of Grandmother's dresses. I enjoyed myself very much and was sorry when the maid came to fetch me home.

When I was five years old, my sister Bianka was born. We were told about this news while we were on our walk back from the local garden. The little sister gave us much pleasure but soon inspired our envy when our father, who was generally serious and strict, paid much more attention to her than to the rest of us.

In the meantime, I was sent to the kindergarten of "Aunt" Jettchen Koppenheim. She had a big hunchback, but all the children loved her. I enjoyed going to this place, as the various games and handcrafts that were there gave me much pleasure. I especially enjoyed making things out of clay. I was especially proud to be able to provide material from my father's brick factory. After we made the saucers, jugs, and other small items, they were dried and the good "aunt" painted them with a golden varnish.

One Saturday afternoon, my mother and I visited Aunt Jettchen. From what I overheard from their conversation, I found out that I was supposed to start to learn to read and to write with this kindergarten teacher. At the end of the school day, I was given special lessons. Within a short time, I was ready to transfer to the next to the highest grade of the so-called Citizens' School, which resulted in a substantial saving of school time.

I reported to that school at Christmastime. I never learned why my Father took these steps. One can assume, however, that as the chairperson of the local town's council, he knew already at Christmastime that by Easter, a Girl's School would open in town. In any case, I was led to an overcrowded classroom run by Mr. Morkowski. The teacher welcomed me in a friendly manner and asked me where in the class I wanted to sit. When I was too embarrassed to reply, he asked the class: "Who amongst you knows the little Herzfeld?" In response, forty hands went up. Apparently, the whole class knew me. I was a bit frightened when the teacher asked me whom I knew and I responded timidly, "Else Rubensohn." Thereupon the teacher asked me to be the fourth student to share Else's table.

The teacher was very nice, but, unfortunately, he was frequently out sick. In his absence, he was replaced by one of the students from the highest grade in the school. This substitute was only slightly successful. I must admit, however, that I was happy to leave the Citizens' School at Easter time with a good report card, and transfer to the Girl's School. Else Rubensohn (the daughter of our family doctor), Frieda Hennig (the daughter of the general manager of the local mill), and I together formed the lowest grade in that school.

Miss Pohl, who managed the school, taught us natural sciences and history. Miss Jablonski, to whom we gave the nickname "Aunt Fanny," taught us all the other subjects.

The first year at the Girls' School was very enjoyable. Miss Pohl took us for a walk every Wednesday in the afternoon, during which she provided us with lessons of natural science. She also made special cookies for us and treated us as if she were our mother.

On one of the Wednesdays, the other girls in the class told Miss Pohl the big secret that my birthday would fall on the following day. When Miss Pohl asked me how old I was going to be, I replied that I was going to be seven years old. She then said with a sigh, "In that case, you are one year too young." On the following day, both teachers appeared with a bag full of candy. This was not repeated in subsequent years, when more students joined the class. Moreover, our relationship with Miss Jablonski soon became cloudy. She was one of those old spinsters who was nervous and irritable. Her ways of expressing herself were violent and without restraint. The students gave her a hard time, and, without exception, all were on a war footing with her. On the other hand, Miss Pohl was always considered and just in her attitude and was generally loved by her students. I remember her fondly.

As I recall, the whole of the first school year passed in a friendly and enjoyable manner. Studying was very easy for me. My handwriting was less than satisfactory, according to both the school and my parents. This did not cause me grief, as my grades were very good and I was satisfied with my accomplishments.

This all changed later on. New students joined the class, who in spirit and action did not improve the situation. Moreover, these girls were bigger than I was, and I had always remained the youngest and one of the weakest in my grade, which allowed these newcomers to terrorize me. The sisters Habeck, two daughters of the owner of a brewery that later on went out of business, were still at the height of their strength at that time. These girls had their own cart and ponies and were given whatever they wanted by their father. Their mother was no longer living at that time. They caused me much pain on several occasions. They were also the cause of an "Unsatisfactory" grade in Behavior, which I was given at that time. This bad note stayed with me for quite some time and was only removed from my record when Miss Pohl became our classroom teacher.

During a Physical Education class, I committed the not too serious "offense" of passing gas. On the way home from school, the elder of the Habeck sisters came from behind me and called me "Rolling Wagon." This annoyed me, of course, and caused us to have a serious fight, in which I unfortunately did not fare well. Our teacher, who was nearby, separated the fighting parties. He also saw to it that all participants were given a stain on their record. The two sisters continued to bother me by calling me names. Life has caused these sisters enough suffering so that the pain they caused me has long been avenged. On the other hand, I remember Else Rubensohn, Lydia Kahk, and several other classmates who proved themselves to be very nice young ladies. We did not become very close friends, but we were good companions.

During the next school years, a set pattern was followed. School vacations always passed in a great hurry. If it were not for occasional visits by relatives, the school holidays and the Jewish holidays were the only break in the routine. The Jewish holidays and Friday evenings were the highlights of our life. Because Fridays were the market days, these days were usually very busy. During my childhood, it frequently happened that the business on that day was so hectic that the children were also asked to help in the store during the afternoon, which we enjoyed very much. On these days, lunch [*normally the main meal of the day*] was taken on the run. Our parents had much to do until evening came and Sabbath began. At this point, all activity ended and Father went to the synagogue, Mother and daughters changed to better dresses, and the eldest daughter present had to cook the fish, without which one could not think of observing the Friday Evening meal.

When Father returned from services, all was ready for a friendly and peaceful family evening. On such evenings even my strict father was lighthearted, and we were allowed to stay at the dinner table and read. Everything was pleasant and friendly on that night. I cannot recall even one case where something unpleasant was said on a Friday night. It was the unwritten law of the house that this night was a holy evening.

Saturday was less festive than Friday night. On that day, the business was closed and we enjoyed eating a "better" midday meal. We ate cakes as part of the morning and evening meals, which had some special meaning for us children. But the children were mostly bored on Saturdays. Out of consideration for the Jewish community, we were not allowed to play the piano on that day, which, as children, we considered a bother.

That we all had to participate in the obligatory Saturday hike was also not appreciated by the children. Nonetheless, Mother insisted that at least once a week, we follow her lead. Even our father had to come on these hikes, regardless of whether he was healthy or sick. As Father had often called for meetings of the town council, of which he served as chairman, for Saturday afternoons, we often found ourselves standing with a coat and hat, ready to go, while waiting for him to join us.

The walk always started by going to Opalenitza, and from there, depending on the weather and Father's wish, we proceeded to either the last or next-to-last stop of the local tram line. Along the way, we usually met the same Jewish residents of the town, with whom we exchanged a brief greeting or a short conversation. These walks were also a sort of parade, in which one showed off one's new clothing. Occasionally we took a long return track through the fields, but, when the path was muddy, which usually was the case, we walked back along the same track on which we had come. On nice summer days or in the spring, we sometimes walked all the way to the "Forest." This was a walk of about three-quarters of an hour along a path in the fields. This was very nice, as we walked along the fields of corn.

At the woods, we rested. For as long as the children were young, we were subjected to a recurring game in which suddenly an apple or orange "appeared" under a fir tree. When I became older, my mother's "adventurousness" reached the point where she took us by train to Urbanowo, which was two stops further out on the tram. There was a forest at that stop, and the local shop sold coffee-like beverages, which one could enjoy outdoors, together with cake that we brought along.

There were never occasions to meet others on these outings, which, I feel, influenced our upbringing. Our father was not lighthearted by nature. Because of his unnatural smartness and his business acumen, there was little social contact between him and those of the community who were deemed worthy of contact. We were told that our parents had participated in and enjoyed lighthearted social contacts during the early days of their marriage and that Father was very lighthearted at that time and took part in theatrical productions. By the time I was a young child, this was all in the past. By then, the families with whom it was felt that it might be nice to visit had either died out or moved away. Those who were still in town were simple people with whom it was not too desirable to spend one's time. Only very few amongst our Christian neighbors were deemed interesting. As a result of this, we grew up in "splendid isolation."

We had frequent visits by people such as Father's partner in the brick factory, a master builder by the name of Gutsche, or Mr. Heinrich Meyer, the owner of a local mill who, I believe, would have liked to become Father's son-in-law (I was not considered! [*meaning "not considered to be a suitable bride"–likely she was too young at the time*]), a lawyer by the name of Mr. Rockau, and several landowners from our neighborhood, among others. We were also visited daily by Mr. Victor Greiffenberg, who wrote his name with a small letter "v." He was very happy when people who did not know him well addressed him as "Herr von Greiffenberg" [*the prefix "von" in a German surname usually indicated nobility*]. He and his wife had no children of their own. They visited us frequently, and there was close contact between them and our parents. The wife was a small woman who always dressed up, and she kept her hair in a most painstaking manner. She was a very nice person, and the children in our house enjoyed her company. The husband was a bit dry. He can best be described by the old saying: "Not a big brain and not a small fool." The poor wife ended her days in an asylum. She probably suffered a lot in her married days, which may have contributed to her going mad. The husband led a rather loose life after the wife was institutionalized, and he also carried on questionable financial dealings.

We did not enjoy a really close contact with other families we considered equal to us. Our father's special position was always pointed out to us. This created an atmosphere of superiority, which I tried not to demonstrate on the outside but which I was unable to overcome internally until much later. I must also admit that one would have mingled with others more easily, had one been more exposed. It could also be that there were no suitable people to befriend, which was why we had few friends as children.

After this lengthy departure from the topic, let me come back and talk about the holidays.

The *Pesach* [*Passover*] holidays were very special. Long before the holidays, we already undertook a major cleanup, as the house had to be cleaned of all things that were considered to be "sour." About eight to fourteen days before the feast, a huge laundry basket was set up with a fresh linen lining, to hold the matzot that were obtained from the baker. Even during our youth, at a time when not everyone was still at home, we needed one hundred kilograms, or even more, of matzot for the eight days of the feast.

On the Sunday before the holiday, a big table was set up in the yard, on which the cakes for the holidays were produced. This had to take place in the yard, as the kitchen was not yet ready for the festival. As one could only obtain little or no Kosher for Pesach butter, the cakes were mostly in the form of biscuits, which incorporated a very large number of eggs, but which seemed to us as children to have a rather dry texture. The macaroons were the most loved item, and they were baked in very large lots. When the flat pans were brought back from the baker, the children tried to sneak a macaroon, which was a great pleasure. The children, especially we girls, always stayed near the place where the cakes were prepared and tried to get a chance to lick the used cooking utensils and spoons.

On the day before Pesach [*Erev Pesach*], all the items that were not allowed to be used during the eight days of the holiday were removed from the house and placed in the basement. This created an opportunity for us to take a bit of such good things as the chocolate that Mother had purchased from a factory in large lots, and which was used primarily in preparing chocolate drinks and the renowned chocolate fish. This chocolate was kept in thick strips. If we were able to break off a corner or crack off a piece, without being seen, that was a real joy.

On the morning of the holiday, we had a hasty breakfast in which we included bread and other fermented items. Then, all the contents of the kitchen were removed and the Pesach cutlery and china were taken out from the storage area and placed in the kitchen. In the meantime, the fire was lit under the stove, and the cooking plate was heated to the point that it was so hot that it had a glowing red color. In doing so, the last traces of *chometz* [*fermented material*] were removed. Only after that was done, could one start cooking for the holidays.

At the same time, Father, equipped with a lantern and accompanied by his sons, scoured the house looking for items that were not allowed during Pesach. He finally located a piece of bread that had been hidden for him, and he burned it, celebrating the "burning of the *chometz*."

At lunchtime during the day of the holiday, we were given Mother's special soup and pureed potatoes with some meat. Officially, matzot were not allowed to be eaten until the Seder. We did, however, find ways to get some before the services.

At long last, the expected evening arrived. In the course of the day, several special plates were prepared for the evening service, which the children observed eagerly. An egg roasted in its shell was placed on one plate. A piece of roasted meat was placed on a second small bowl. Some ground horseradish was placed in another bowl, and bite-sized salad leaves were placed in the next. *Charoset*, the symbol of clay, which was made out of apple, nuts, cinnamon, and other delicacies, was placed in another bowl. Father, who owned a brick factory, always asked the children in the course of the evening service to calculate how much it would cost to make one thousand bricks from this mix.

A very festive table was prepared for the evening, with silver cutlery and porcelain plates and wine glasses for all attendees. Only Father was given the silver cup that was traditionally used for the Shabbat service. He was also provided with the plush seat from the visiting room and the *kippa* [*head cover or yarmulke*] with the silver embroidery. He was dressed in the special white shirt that we called the Dead Man's Shirt. After the service we sat down, and Mother, who usually wore a black dress, was dressed for this evening in a petite white apron.

The Seder evening was celebrated very seriously and with everyone paying attention to the story. Only when we reached the second part of the evening with the singing of "Chad Gadja" and the other songs did the evening become lighter-hearted. As a child, I found it sometimes difficult to stay in focus, as I was reading the German translation of the story and was, therefore, finished before Father, who read the Hebrew version and then translated it, while adding his commentary. When the first part of the service with its many ceremonies and prayers came to an end, the actual meal finally began. My brothers enjoyed emptying the wine glasses when the appropriate prayers called for a drink. All were served real Hungarian wine on this occasion; the choice was between sweet and dry wines. As a result, some of the youngsters were drunk under the table before the evening was over.

Originally, the meal of the first Seder evening consisted of Mother's special bouillon with eggs, a roasted piece of meat and stewed fruit. On the second Seder night we had fish as the main course. After Father teased Mother one year saying: "At MY Mother's house we had fish AND meat on the first night of the Seder," our mother also prepared both dishes for that night. This turned the holiday dinner into a major attack on one's stomach. In spite of this, I consider the first Seder nights as some of my nicest childhood memories. It had a glow and festivity that is hard to define. The fact that the young assistants from the business were also all present at our table on that night did not distract from the evening but rather added a nice Jewish spirit to the evening. At the end of the meal, Father would pronounce in a strong voice, *"Le schone habo in Graetz"* [*"next year in Graetz"*]. He was not a Zionist!

The second Seder night was much more subdued. Father read a shorter version of the story without adding his explanations, so the special spirit of the first night was missing. Although my parents knew this version of the Seder was not really the same, they would have considered it a sin to skip the second night.

The Pesach week also differed in many other ways from the rest of the year. As fewer ingredients were available for use in cooking the meals during this week, the allowed materials were incorporated in special ways. We had more meat and more eggs than was usually the custom. With eggs, a special "covered matzo" was prepared, which the children loved. We also had the opportunity to eat first at the house of Grandfather, who took his meal at noon. We then ate again at Aunt Roeschen Stern's house, and finally we devoured cakes, made of eggs, at our own home. We never felt that this was too much food, nor did we ever make comparisons to figure out who made the best version of the meal, although, without doubt, our mother's cooking was the best of the three. She never let the kitchen help cook these holiday items, and she was even reluctant to let her daughters take over this duty.

I must add a word about *chrimsel* [*matzot with egg sugar and raisins fried in butter*]. Even at that era, when food was rich in fat, this dish was in a class by itself, which is saying a lot. As with all diversions, especially in the case of youngsters, we could hardly wait for the end of the holiday, which signaled the end of these delicacies. The first warm bread at the end of the holiday was eaten as if we had been starving. Then the regular routine resumed.

The other holidays also had their symbolism and traditions. As children, we appreciated the culinary traditions related to these feasts. However, none of them reached the peaks of the Pesach days. Our dear mother was glad when the holidays were over, as they had meant much additional effort and extra work for her.

I have so far written very little about the grandparents. I only got to know well my Grandfather Herzfeld and Grandmother Badt. I only have a dim recollection of Grandmother Herzfeld. She sat quietly in her corner and in her last years was said to have been somewhat odd or strange. Grandfather Badt died when I was five years old, but I cannot recall having met him.

Grandfather Herzfeld, who lived in Graetz, was loved by all the children. He died at the age of eighty, when I was nine years old. He was a very religious but also a very tolerant man. He was a small person with a fine and spiritually rich face. Every Saturday after school, the children would come to his house. He would talk to us for a while and then he gave each of us his blessing and a piece of sweet cake. That was a hard and fast rule. I can say with certainty that the blessing was more important for us than the cake. Without exaggeration, I know that seldom in my later years did I feel such a rapt atmosphere as during these blessings, while we were kneeling in front of this honorable figure.

After the blessings, we were then sent to Emilie, who was in the kitchen. She was his elderly caregiver who formerly was the children's supervisor and who now assisted Cousin Helene

Breslauer in running the household. Emilie always had something small for the visiting children.

During the Purim holidays, Emilie made wonderful ginger nut cookies. For Purim, the children were also given costumes. We then went from house to house to beg for sweets. People wearing masks always disturbed me. At home we had the traditional *kreppchehen* [*doughnuts*] for lunch on Purim, and in the evening we were given a diluted punch drink, which, as children, we regarded as something special.

We saw Grandfather primarily at his home or on the way to or from the synagogue. As a result, it was a real surprise for me to meet him on a summer day walking in a passageway in the field with his friend Reb Gabriel Hirsch. I was with a couple of school friends and could not get home fast enough with the news. That was, however, his last hike in the countryside. Not long after that, this gentle man started getting ill. He suffered for a while from pain, and he died a few days after my ninth birthday.

Nothing hurt me more as a youngster than an event that took place during that time, with one of my aunts. We knew as children that Grandfather was not well. Something drove me on that day to his house. I stood on the upper floor of the house of the aunt with whom Grandfather Herzfeld was staying. I waited in the hope that I could see him for a minute. The aunt came from his room and when she saw me, she said: "Go home; you'll get your Taler." Truthfully, I did not even consider the birthday gift, and I was insulted at her limited understanding of my feelings for my grandfather that had brought me there. I did, however, get to see him through the cracks, and I composed a lengthy ballad about the "Influenza," which we intended to send to him through the door, and so I left the house.

Grandfather's funeral took place with much honor and respect, at the synagogue. This was the first funeral I had ever attended. In addition to the feeling of sorrow, there was a feeling of fulfillment seeing that my grandfather was sent off with such honor and accompanied by so many people.

As children, we remembered Grandmother Badt, who lived in Posen, best of all grandparents. Almost until the time of my engagement, she had visited us frequently and took over whenever our mother went on a trip to a resort. She was rather strict and did not allow any foolhearted behavior or laziness. But she was the embodiment of goodness. Her whole pleasure was in giving and gifting. She had no selfish needs and had more of an understanding of the younger generation than did her much-younger daughter [*Julie*].

In addition to the 2 Talers that each of us received in our savings account on our birthdays, Grandmother Badt always added a Mark [*a smaller coin*] for free spending. This was a real treasure for us, as we were always short of free pocket money. When this extra Mark also ended up in the savings account, Grandmother added a small gift, such as a pair of gloves made of yarn. When we came to Posen for a visit, she always had something nice as a gift. When I traveled to Posen more frequently, as an older girl, Grandmother always gave me 3 Marks and said: "Buy yourself a nice bow or something else for yourself, something that your mother would not have wanted to see on your travel expenses."

Grandmother lived in the home of Aunt Jenny Krombach and helped her in running her home, as the aunt was busy helping in her husband's business. She also took care of the aunt's children. The oldest child of my aunt was Hella [*Krombach*]. She was a year younger than I and she was supposed to be a model child. The best way to create envy between relatives is to set one as a model to the other. This happened often enough between us, resulting in my disliking Hella intensely. When my father returned from Posen, he always said; "Hella is such a competent girl. She always wears her kitchen apron." This argument did not convince me that Hella was competent. Later on I found out that she was a nice girl, who never did anything to harm anyone. As young children, however, we could not stand one another.

During one of the times that Grandmother was in Graetz, while our mother was in Karlsbad on one of her trips, the following happened. Our yard was surrounded by a fence made of iron rods. My brother Ernst was fencing with a friend, while I was sitting on a box and watching them. Suddenly one of the iron bars fell on my head. Not much would have happened to me had the iron bar hit me flat on my head. I did, however, run away from the falling bar in the direction of a piece of farm machinery. This resulted in a serious head wound. Grandmother was very worried and concerned that the injury occurred while she was in charge. On the other hand, I was proud at the fact that I took it well and was a bit disappointed that the wound did not require stitching. My brothers had had such injuries in the past, and I was disappointed that they never happened to me.

The biggest event of my youth was the engagement and wedding of my sister Rosa. Mother and Rosa had frequently traveled to Posen for shopping. Mother was always in a great hurry to return home, but she let Rosa stay longer in Posen. On a nice summer day Mother came back home alone. On the following day she was busy fixing my sister Bianka's and my dresses. As we were on the school holidays, we were home when Rosa came from the train station with a basket full of flowers. To Mother's question she replied, "It is from him." A few days later, as I was walking back from school, I met our father, together with a friendly looking gentleman, whom he led to the local hotel. During lunch, the gentleman was introduced to us as "Uncle Hugo," a nephew of my father who had suddenly turned up. This appeared to me to be rather farfetched. In spite of the fact that everything at home was arranged in a festive way, I did not figure out the real situation.

A few days after that, while we were already on summer vacation, we had with us our younger nephew Leo Mielziner and a Jewish child from Posen who came to spend the vacation with us. The five children and the caregiver were given an early lunch at twelve noon, and we were then sent to a small park, which was near our home. It was a very hot day, and we had no desire to play outdoors. We only had some cucumbers to chew and we lay around on a bench in the "summer house" that was in that garden.

At three o'clock, we were summoned back home, dressed in good clothing and taken to Rosa's room. There, the young pair was introduced to us as a couple and the intended groom produced a large basket full of candy, which, as the eldest in the group, I accepted. Then we were allowed to greet Papa and Mama Brodnitz, Grete, Selma, and Julius. Each of us gave them a sharp bow, and we also gave each a kiss. I was subjected to a lot of teasing, as I also gave Julius a kiss. After that, we were allowed to depart. I don't recall it but, according to the tale that Julius Brodnitz told later on, I proceeded to divide the confections by saying, "One for you, one for you, one for you, and one for me." I do know for certain that my mother asked on the following day about the expensive candy but that it was all gone.

As the intended groom, Hugo came every other Sunday to visit us in Graetz, and soon we all loved him. With the exception of Bianka, we soon dropped the "uncle" part of his name. She was still so young that for a long time she called all of Hugo's siblings, including her future husband, "Uncle" and "Aunt."

On one of his first visits, Hugo came with a small suitcase full of gifts for all the children. Both Bianka and I were given an armband made of silver. The high point of my joy on that occasion was the fact that mine also had a little heart attached to it! Poor Rosa did not have an easy time while she was engaged.

We had summer vacation and all the children were at home. We also had many guests. However, things were not always peaceful between Cousin Lenchen Badt, who was staying with us for weeks at a time and Lenchen Herzfeld, who had a very energetic temper. Lenchen Badt always thought that she had to correct and educate us, the other children. She also was the cause of a nasty occurrence.

Hugo usually visited on Sundays, arriving at noon, and he left in the evening by coach to Opalenitza, where he caught the last train of the evening to Posen. In order to catch that train, he had to leave Graetz at nine forty-five in the evening. As we ate our evening meal early, there was another serving, without the children, at nine, in which the adults got tea and a piece of pastry.

On one such evening, we accompanied our future in-law, Hugo, to the door of our house. I turned back before the others. This led Cousin Lenchen [*Badt*] to make the false claim that I had gone back to sneak a piece of the pastry and some candy. As it was already too late for someone who was, at the time, only eleven years old, the inquiry about her claim did not take place on that evening. On the following morning, L. B. [*Lenchen Badt*] brought up her claim again. As I refused to "admit" to the charge, she convinced Rosa that I should not be allowed to eat the first or second breakfast. This game was supposed to continue over lunch, but my father, who only found out about this charge at that time, intervened (Mother was away from home at Karlsbad). He just said, "It's all right—just sit down and join in the meal."

Such and similar occurrences did not endear L. B. amongst us. We were all relieved when she left after a stay of six weeks in our home, a time that appeared to us as endless. We never had any problems with Rosa. She just could not rid herself of the influence of L. B. Things returned to normal after L. B. left.

A few weeks before Rosa's wedding, I had the rare good luck of being held out of school for a day. I was taken to Posen in order to be "equipped." My wardrobe was so badly in need of refreshing that I needed to borrow a hat from Lenchen [*Herzfeld, her sister*] and a pair of woolen gloves from my brother Hugo. I remember the gloves in particular, as they were tight on me.

When we visited, with Rosa, the home of the elder Brodnitz family in Posen, I was given a piece of pastry. This caused me some embarrassment when I tried to take off the gloves. I hope that no one noticed that I hastily had to use my teeth to get the gloves off. The friendly and kind way in which the elder Brodnitzes received us and the distinguished way in which they were living (for those days), made a deep impression on me. During those days, I was given many things of special elegance. The grandmother declared, jokingly, that I should be wearing the new blue outfit only when there were holidays that lasted for three days. (This, as everyone knows, is never the case.) I was in seventh heaven when all these wonderful items arrived and all fit well.

The wedding of Hugo and Rosa! That was a feast that shed its light on our youth for a long time. The memories of that event have long lived with us. As both Hugo and Rosa were the oldest children in their families, their wedding became a public festival in which all the relatives took part. Not fewer than about one hundred people turned up for the occasion. On the evening before the wedding, the poor guests had to listen to numerous poems and other readings by the four Herzfeld kids (Lenchen also took part in the production, while Ernst stayed in reserve). Several of the Krombach children, those who were old enough to speak, also participated. In the morning of the wedding day, Paul Brodnitz, who insisted on being called "Uncle," took us children for a walk together with Lenchen. We ended up in the new apartment of the new couple, which was on Kanonenplatz. The place was almost ready and seemed to us to be very fine indeed. Paul ate breakfast with Lenchen, Bianka, and me, and he gave us nice gifts.

The wedding ceremony affected me so much that I started to sob. When they tried to comfort me I said: "You can laugh, as you are getting Rosa, while we are losing her now." After the ceremony the general jolly spirit returned. I was very pleased when the brothers of Hugo and some of the other men addressed me as "Miss Hedwig." I had a real gentleman as the table master (Hermann) and was allowed to sit at the grownups' table. Together with my brother Hugo, I came into the hall, riding on a toy train, and handed out posies to the ladies. All were very kind to me. For those of us who took part in such an event for the first time, this whole affair had the feeling of a fairy tale. We found this entire event, with its special food and ice cream, unbelievably nice. Julius danced a farmer's dance with Grete and Selma, while dressed in a costume. Already then, I thought he was especially attractive and distinguished. Of all of Hugo's brothers I liked him best, although it was in a way that one likes a pretty picture. Some people claimed later on that Mama Brodnitz had told my mother at that time, "Save Hedwig for my Julius." However, I am not sure this was not invented at a later date.

Even this nice festivity had to come to an end. On the following day, we all traveled back home. For a long period after this event, our schoolmates were hearing stories about the wedding from us.

At the beginning of January, the young couple returned from their honeymoon trip. Mother went to Posen to greet them and returned home as the first one in our family to have come down with a strong case of influenza. This was the time when the first nasty influenza infection spread throughout the world. Everyone was forced to stay in their sickbed. In our household, the infection went down the line through all members of the family. Our Christmas school vacation was extended by fourteen days. Hugo and I together composed a lengthy "Ballad of the Influenza," which we intended to send to a humorous publication. Unfortunately this creative effort was lost without a trace.

When summer arrived that year, we made a school trip to Posen! This gave me the opportunity to visit Rosa for the first time in her new home. Both she and Adolfine Brodnitz, who picked me up for the meal, were very kind to me. After the meal, I met up with my classmates at the local zoo. We were also shown the cathedral, the Radzynski Library, the army's headquarters, Wilhelm's Place, and many other points of interest. That evening we traveled back home, very tired but feeling we'd had a wonderful day.

Shortly after that trip, our school holidays began. I was invited to Schrimm to visit our relatives, the Breslauers, while Bianka was invited to stay with Rosa in Posen, where she enjoyed a wonderful stay. As she later told me, she was allowed to wear her new red muslin dress every day. "Uncle Hermann" took her daily to a bakery for sweet goods. My stay in Schrimm was not as lush as this, but I had, nonetheless, a great time during the visit. Aunt Breslauer and Aunt Stern both were sisters of my father. They were both very cheerful and good natured.

I stayed with the Breslauers, where two of the daughters were approximately my age, and we had a very enjoyable time. Just bathing in the cold waters of the river Warthe was a new experience for me, as we had no such opportunities in Graetz. Recha and Trude Breslauer had many girlfriends. With these girls and their brothers, we undertook beautiful hikes every day and practiced a little harmless flirting. The aunts had an understanding for our acts, which our mother, who was always serious and overburdened by duty, never really achieved. The aunts enjoyed little pleasures and allowed some small deviations. As a result, I enjoyed myself there, and on the following year, I was excited to be able to go there again. That time around the "older nephew" Benno Stern was also there, and he was especially nice to me. Near the end of the vacation, I was suddenly given the order from home to leave early and stop over in Posen. I was to see a throat and nose specialist, as I had been subject to frequent attacks of cold germs. I was rather annoyed about this, as I would have preferred to stay longer in Schrimm with the Breslauers. But nothing helped, and I had to leave.

Dr. Lichtenstein in Posen took a few stabs at it but suggested I come back in the fall for a longer treatment. As my parents agreed with this proposal, I left only to return at the agreed time to Posen. My siblings had, however, more confidence in a Dr. Korach and brought me to his clinic. I am now convinced that the specialist could have made things much easier for me. In any case, the treatment lasted all through the fall vacation and then continued for a few more days, while school was back in session. This was followed by another stay with Rosa in Posen, during the Christmas holidays. The treatment resulted in considerable pain and discomfort but I was also able to have a good time as a result of it.

During this time in Posen, I had my first chance to go to the theater. This was followed a short time later by several additional opportunities to see shows. The first visit was when I went to see *The Magic Flute*, for which I thank my future mother-in-law. Her good intentions were slightly spoiled when she said, "This is the show to which one goes with children, when they go to the theater for the first time." I, at the age of thirteen, thought of myself as being well past the childhood stage. I enjoyed the music very much and thought highly of the whole performance. When I came back during the Christmas holidays, Hugo and Rosa took me several times to the theater. The one that left the strongest lasting impression on me was the winning performance of *Cavalleria*. I also remember fondly the performance of *The Puppet Fairy*.

On the occasion of this trip to Posen, I received a new dress that, in line with the fashion of Posen at that time, was decorated with many golden bars. That resulted in teasing by my uncle Simon Krombach, who always knew how to talk to children.

He repeatedly asked me when I had earned the bars of a non-commissioned officer. Later, when Hugo was bar mitzvahed, this uncle gave him much pleasure by asking him every five minutes what time it was. This gave Hugo the opportunity to show off his new watch.

I had to spend a lot of time at the doctor's office and was not allowed to go out much. My relatives, especially Hugo and Rosa, were very kind to me. Hugo wanted to get a Christmas tree for me. At the end this did not happen, out of consideration for my mother, who joined us for the Christmas holidays. This trip was the last one I took for the next two years, during which I seldom traveled and then only briefly to Posen. The next major event in our lives was the rebuilding of our home.

The original old family home, which was built by Grandfather Herzfeld as a two-story house, had long been too small for our family. On the ground floor, it had the store and two rooms on either side of the hallway. Similarly, it had two rooms on the left and the right of the stairs on the second floor. The rooms on the upper floor had a rather low ceiling. The largest of these rooms was used as the living room and was officially called "The Lower Parlor." A small room with one window was connected to the parlor. This was used by my parents as their bedroom. For as long as I can recall, the rooms on the other side of the stairs on both floors were used as storage areas for the business. One of the storage rooms on the upper level was designed, in a manner that I never understood, in a way that allowed its ceiling to be rolled up so that we could build a sukkah for the holidays of the tabernacle. During the Sukkot holidays, the children were given the assignment of decorating the place with chains of chestnut leaves and other plants.

My grandparents had lived in the house, together with my parents, for many years. They moved out, some time ago, when the place became too small for our growing family. Over a period of time, my father purchased two adjacent properties and he then tore down their existing structures. He next built additions to the house on these properties. As a result of this step-by-step construction, our home became larger but not very practical. On the ground floor we had the store, an office, and a large but dark dining room. In addition, we had a kitchen and a very large wash room that also served as a primitive bathroom for that level. That room also contained a pump that provided the house with water, which, in those days, was considered a unique feature that was seldom seen. There was also a winding staircase from that room to the second floor. The main staircase, which was well lit, was seldom used by members of the family. On the second level were two rooms for the children, a bedroom for our parents, and the "Good Chamber" and "The Lower Parlor." In between was the narrow room that, as I had mentioned before, was used as the room for visitors.

Half of the rooms were, however, rather dark. They faced a glass-covered yard. This glass ceiling was on rollers, and it was frequently pushed aside during the summer months. During the winter it always stayed closed, as the yard contained large stocks of iron rods, which had to be protected against moisture or wetness. This setup caused the airing of the rooms that faced the yard to be less than ideal. As we were accustomed to these conditions, one did not complain. Moreover, we were rather healthy in spite of it all.

There was no supply of running water in our town. As mentioned before, we had our own pump and did not have to fetch the water from the water hole down the street. This was considered a great comfort in those days. The "toilettes" were located a bit further in the yard, but they were completely protected from the elements. As the yard was enclosed, we could use the facilities even in bad weather without having to suffer from either a cold draft or rain. I believe that in such small towns, the hygienic conditions have not improved all that much even to the present day.

Our father had built the house by himself. With proper guidance, the building could probably have been designed better. This can also be said of some of the other buildings of that time. My father's partner in the brick factory, a man by the name of Mr. Gutsche, claimed to be a master builder. I think he was not much of a construction expert. He prided himself on having designed a special front to the building of a type that had not yet been seen in Graetz at that time. In terms of practical use of the space, he had little to offer.

The old house with its many corners, roof chambers and cellar rooms was a paradise as a play area for us children. The way to the roof was a special pleasure for us. The addition had a flat roof without a gable. From one of the rooms we could, however, climb to the roof. As girls, we found this to be a bit frightening, but we participated in it nonetheless. On the ground floor there were many secret corners filled with old junk, where, as children, we always found some treasures, which caused us to be sorry to leave the old place.

I have several remembrances related to the old house.

There were three granite steps in the stoop, which we used for fun and games. (Ernst had these steps to thank for the scar on his forehead.) The store also always held attraction for us children. Ernst's confirmation took place in the old house, but I don't remember much about this event. I do remember, however, that in honor of our mother, we got a new lamp with five flames for the "Good Room." The room was also supposed to have the head of a deer, which was mounted on ebony wood. This special piece caused a delay in our moving into the new house, as it was not ready in time.

From the time before we moved to the new house, I also remember a few events. After Father completed the second addition to the old house, Ernst, Lenchen, and I, together with our brave supervisor, Josefa, were sitting at a table in the children's room under a hanging burning oil lamp. I was very tired and propped my head on the table, while Ernst and Lenchen were doing some school work. Suddenly the lamp came crashing down and broke on the table. The fuel spread on the table and the flame followed all over the table and to the books that were on it. I was moved by the maid to a corner of the room, and, in response to our yelling, our mother rushed from the kitchen with her hands covered with dough. She first gave each of the children a solid smack on the cheek and then took off her kitchen apron and put out the fire. We could not figure out what had caused the lamp to come down. Lenchen said she thought I had pulled on the lamp, but Josefa contradicted this.

I also recall some events that took place at that time. Our mother had traveled on a *Kur* [*cure*] to Karlsbad. She had very poor health and, in spite of that, ran the house and the business. Her poor body from time to time failed her. I can still see her sitting on the leather sofa in the business, doubled over in pain, while waiting for the pain to subside. She had no time to be sick except, perhaps, on Saturday mornings. Even on that day, there were many tasks awaiting her that she believed she alone could handle. So, even Saturdays were not really days of rest for her. She set very high standards for herself, and her expectations from her children were also not small. From early on, everyone was expected to do his assigned duties.

Although we sometimes complained and rebelled secretly against these expectations, later in life we thanked her and our father a thousand times over for instilling in us this sense of duty.

As young as I was at that time, I was sometimes bitter when I had to help in the sewing, while my friends could go on a hike. Mother's annual rehabilitation trips took place usually during the school holidays in the summer, as the business was relatively slow during the harvest time. My brothers were also at home during the school holidays. One day, while I was sitting on the stairs in the upper level, I heard major shouting going on upstairs. Father called from the ground level to keep quiet. When nothing happened he came rushing in a great hurry up the stairs, where he saw me first. He gave each of us a smack in the face, without first inquiring what was going on. This was the only time that I ever recall getting hit by my father. The fact that it was unjustified caused me to never forget it.

From time to time, father took us along on his weekly trips to the brick factories. He would rent a wagon that could accommodate four people. When his partner Gutsche declined to come on the trip, several seats were available for the children. My brothers used these opportunities regularly. For me this pleasure was rather questionable because I could not stand riding facing backward. When I could not sit facing the front or sitting next to the coachman, I declined the offer. The place of honor, which was sitting facing the front, seldom fell my way, and mother did not want the girls to sit on the back bench.

One day Ernst, Lenchen, and I were traveling with our father. Lenchen was so kind as to give me the seat that was facing forward. It was during the season of the sour cherries. In the first brick factory, there was a row of cherry trees. The wife of the manager of the brick factory prepared coffee for us. She was always very kind to us children. When she expected the children to come along, she prepared Fruit Eggs. Eggs were cooked together with onion peels and they got some fruit colors. She would hide them under the trees, and we were sent out to look for them. This time, however we made ourselves comfortable under the low trees and ate a bit too much. When we went on our way to the next brick factory, in spite of the fact that I had the place of honor, I became sick and the following took place: my brother Ernst, who was sitting across from me, started yelling, "Blood, Blood." To this my father responded without getting excited, "Sit quietly—these are only cherry stains."

In the coming period, I almost never visited this brick factory again because I was always reminded of this episode. Years later, when the whole family traveled to this factory, I stayed back and had the honorable assignment to guard the home and business. Suddenly a frightful storm opened up on us. I saw to it that all the windows and external openings were closed, when I remembered that my parents and siblings were at that time sitting in an open cart on the road. I was glad when they turned up, unharmed.

After this long deviation, I would like to come back and tell about the "New House" [*see pictures of the old and new house on page 30*]. In order to allow for the construction of the new house, we had to move both the home and the business for at least half a year. The house across the street from our home also belonged to my parents. It contained a mill and a sweet goods business, which was run by a man who had already declared bankruptcy. The business was, therefore, run under his wife's name and later, under the name of their son. These people were not financially well off. Although Father attempted to write the last rental contract in a generous manner, it resulted in a major fight when he needed the place for his own family for half a year. Father pursued this eviction with great vigor, and at long last the moving of our business began.

The children helped in moving the store with great enthusiasm, and we had a lot of fun. Moving the household was less pleasant for us, and it was especially hard on Mother. The window of the office in the old building was enlarged and it became a door. At this point, a back and forth race began across the street. Poor suffering mother, who maintained the books for the business and kept the bills in the office, had all her documents in the building across the street.

Tearing down the old building caused a lot of dust and dirt, even though all the openings in the wall were generally sealed. As all the rooms were crowded with furniture from the old home, we could not entertain visitors during the building period. Although the construction period resulted in many limitations for the children, we enjoyed that time nonetheless. In spite of instructions to stay out of the construction area, we were always there. The porch on the new house was the first one of its kind in Graetz, and it was of special interest to us.

During the construction period, a bishop or archbishop from Posen came to visit our town. The Polish population, which was Catholic, was all excited. They built special arches along the street, and the houses along the way were festooned and covered with carpets. Our half-finished house had wooden planks on the side that faced the street, which some people considered to be an eye-sore. Several of the Catholic citizens of the town came to my father and asked his permission to put some carpets on the side of the building that was facing the street. This he could not refuse. The parade included bell ringers who were accompanied by musicians. The parade featured pictures of saints and religious flags of the various organizations. In short, it was a demonstration of the Catholic Church's ability to generate public honor for its members.

The whole crowd was on its feet. We sat on what would be, in the future, our new balcony. This was not without some danger, as the cement on the floor was not yet dry. I can see in front of my eyes the young girl who was jumping up and down along the street while yelling in Polish, "Long live our Master, the Archbishop." It was as if the people were almost in a state of drunkenness.

Our new home grew until, before too long, the roof trusses were ready. At that point we celebrated the occasion with a good spread. Large quantities of open-faced sandwiches were prepared for the construction crew. (These sandwiches were made with lard and non-kosher sausages. They were prepared in the yard and put on tables so that none of it would come into the house). The workers were also served large amounts of alcoholic beverages and beer. The master builder [*the foreman*] was invited to our home for a festive breakfast at which he was served Hungarian wine.

This was the end of the big construction. The work on the details inside had only started at that point. The business was moved into the new structure during the fall. The other rooms were not occupied during the following winter, in order to allow the place to dry more completely.

The shop was located in a very large room that had two showcases facing the main street and another window, which was facing the side street. It was a very impressive structure for Graetz. The floor was tiled with stones that were a cross between marble and stone (called "terrazzo"). The tables were also made of a similar stone. The store also had a high ceiling, and it was well lit. In fact, the ceiling was too high so that it was extremely cold during the winter. Mother's frequent stays in the cold store probably exacerbated the lung pains from which she was suffering. The shelves in the store were new and pretty so that the business made a very respectable impression. There were no longer steps from the street into the store. Instead of that, there were now three steps from the shop into the office. Similar steps led from the main floor of the house into the kitchen. All in all, our house was a collection of stairs and steps.

On the ground floor on the other side of the building there were two rooms, one smaller and one larger. They were used as storage areas until the store was sold. After the sale of the store, these rooms were converted into office space. The front door of the house contained several large glass plates. These pieces of glass were protected by a metallic design. A wide staircase led to the second level. A door in the hallway separated the floor from the staircase. In the middle was a spacious hall from which a door led to the loggia. A second door opened to the parents' bedroom walk-in closet. The third door led to the old bedroom (of course, this one also included a step), and a fourth door finally led one into the hall.

This hall was a very large room, and it had four windows, and it reflected the builders' desire to decorate the place. A large ceramic oven with a false fireplace was standing in one corner of the room. The ceiling was loaded with pieces, the wooden doors were made with carvings, and the floor was made of wood planks. The tablecloth, oven, and wallpaper were all made of very colorful materials. No cost savings were attempted on anything in that room. Based on our unspoiled taste and that of our friends, the place appeared to all to be extremely nice and pretty. For as long as this hall was empty, I used it frequently. When I had to memorize long passages, it was very nice to learn them while pacing back and forth in the large room. For example, when I studied my lessons in physics or when poems had to be memorized or when new vocabulary had to be absorbed, all were learned in that room. During the winter, a stove was frequently burning in that room. This was supposed to help dry up the room. I don't know whether or not it was very healthy to be in that room at that time. I never talked much about it, and it, apparently, did not do me any harm.

The whole spring of 1892 was spent on having the new place painted and wallpapered. When mother went on her annual trip to Karlsbad, she stopped in Berlin on the way back, where she ordered the contents of the hall and the new bedroom. She paid for one of these purchases (I do not know which one) from her own savings account, as our father, who had made a major investment in the house, did not want to spend even more.

Next we were visited by a furniture dealer from Berlin. He brought with him drawings and fabric samples. To the extent that the children were allowed to view all this, we were amazed by the splendor of all that we were able to see. Our eyes opened even wider when the items arrived, together with the people who had to assemble them and put them in their assigned places. The furniture, which was covered with red silken fabric and plush green decorations, was especially appreciated. The windows were decorated with fabric and plush material. In the future we often complained when we had the task of brushing and beating the curtains, which appeared to be endlessly long. A very large carpet from Smyrna covered the wooden floor. A petroleum lamp, made out of bronze, with five arms, provided light for the room. In all of Graetz, there was no other room of even remotely similar elegance.

All was ready for the Jewish holidays in the fall. At that time everyone came to congratulate the parents on finishing the new house. Even Miss Jablonski, my former teacher, came with her mother, sat stiffly for half an hour, and conversed with my parents in her stilted manner. As she was departing, she turned at the doorway and said: "Truly, this place is very pretty." We children had a hard time keeping from bursting out in laughter.

The Silver Anniversary of my parents was the first celebration in the new house on October 30, 1892. Grandmother Badt, who was the guest of honor, came to visit a short while before the day and actively helped with the preparations for the event. Most of my parents' siblings, a number of married or at least grownup nephews and nieces, and many friends from Graetz and of course all their children were there. All in all, there were at least fifty people present for the big celebration. The meal was served in the new big hall, and during that time Hugo, Bianka, and I read some rhymes that we had written especially for the occasion. After the meal there was some dancing. This created a rather unusual picture for us children. We saw our parents dancing, which was rather uncommon, especially when our father led a chain dance that stretched out throughout the entire floor. It was a wonderful celebration in which we also ate cakes and drank coffee, and it lasted into the night. Father was given important awards and recognitions from the Town Council, the synagogue, the discount savings bank, and several corporations. Some of the relatives and friends gave my parents gifts, and Father was also awarded a large silver cup.

When the visitors left on the following day, we realized that too much wax had been applied to the new wooden floor. The dancing forced out this wax, which stayed on the floor in the form of small clumps. The call came up: "All men, or rather, all women, up to work." The hired help and all the daughters spent a full day on our knees and worked on the floor with steel wool until it was white and clean once again.

The same winter saw the formation of the Graetzer Aktienbrauerei [*the Graetz Brewing Company*]. This event came about as the result of my father's effort and direction. It brought with it a lot of extra work for my father. The formation of the brewery involved a Jewish chemist who came from outside of our area. This man, whose name was Dr. Papilski, now came frequently to Graetz. This man was strictly observant. He knew how to work his schedule in such a way that resulted in him staying with us for the noon and evening meals. As a result of this, our well-meaning mother could not help but invite him to join us for the meals. My sisters and I disliked him, especially since he never even thanked our mother or brought her even a small gift of appreciation.

Soon my school years came to an end. Previously, when Lenchen was away, I had helped my mother with small tasks around the house. The mid-afternoon snacks were my specialty. That meant I had to prepare a mountain of buttered rolls for all the people in the house and in the shop. Serving a smaller quantity of rolls during the evening was also my responsibility, as well as some other small tasks around the house.

I graduated from school during Easter but was not scheduled to go to Berlin until the following fall. This raised the question as to what I should be doing during this half year while still at home but out of school. Miss Pohl stated that she was ready to give me lessons in language and literature, and I requested that Dr. Lohrer should continue teaching me physics and chemistry. My mother's opinion was that there was plenty for me to do in helping her run the household.

The school year came to an end. Else Rubensohn and I were the first students who had been in the school ever since it was created and who had studied all the grades in it. Miss Pohl, who was always friendly, well meaning, and just, gave the graduation a special flavor. We all shed tears as we received our final report cards. For the first time, my reports were very excellent. We also exchanged little cards with little messages, and we were considered, for the first time, as grown up. Naturally, as part of the graduation we had taken parting pictures (of the five of us). In this picture, which I still have, we look like a group of idiots. We were happy to have the school days behind us, but we took with us many nice memories of our school days.

We had special joy in the last two years of school from lessons given by Dr. Lohrer. He was a young teacher who was married. As a new teacher, he had taught at the Boys' School and was able to get all the young students involved in his lessons. He created a special group amongst the students, which was equipped with drums and pipes. He frequently went hiking with the boys, which we girls were occasionally invited to join. He knew how to make the lessons for both groups of students interesting and attractive.

He taught the higher grades of the Girls' School physics, chemistry, and some anthropology. I have him to thank for the little that I still remember about these topics to this day. He addressed his girl-students with the adult personal pronoun *"Sie"* and when he saw them on the street, greeted them from afar. This was in sharp contrast with the way in which Dr. Sachs had treated us. Dr. Sachs had been a substitute for Miss Pohl when she was out sick. He had taught us English and French for half a year, but he had treated us as silly youngsters. Dr. Lohrer was our idol, and his wife, too, joined us in our respect for him. Dr. Lohrer and Miss Pohl were the best teachers during my school years.

I have already told about the nervous and undisciplined ways of Miss Jablonski. There was also Miss Reimer, whom we liked at first, especially as she had blond hair and blue eyes. We soon lost all respect for her when we realized she had made frequent mistakes. Before too long, we realized that her life after work was not very respectable. She was on the constant hunt for men until she was, at last, successful. Finally there was Miss Crohn, who did not harm anyone but who was so bland that she had no impact on us.

I have not yet said anything about my religious education. Cantor Soboti taught me my first lessons in Hebrew. He was a very courageous man who had a great beard. He came to our home to give the lessons. I was fascinated by the way he would sit facing forward, while his one knee was shaking. Later I went to the community's religious school. Our classes lasted two hours every Wednesday afternoon and every Sunday morning. Our teacher was an elderly man by the name of Mr. Horwitz. He always held a small stick, which he used only when he was made very angry. He was noticeable in that a piece of his undergarments always was visible or that some of his buttons were not properly closed.

In the last years we were taught by Rabbi Dr. Friedmann, who was a nice and well-educated scholar. He taught us Jewish history, whereas until that time we had been taught only to read Hebrew and to translate to and from it, which I found boring. I did, however, learn to translate the main prayers without effort, and I could also write German using Hebrew letters. Our grandmother thought it was very important that we could write our holiday greetings and New Year's cards to her in Hebrew.

Before I continue with my recollections of my youth, I would like to add a few other memories from that period. As I have already mentioned, our life was very quiet in our protected nest. Life proceeded along on a very even keel. Therefore, any change from the routine was very welcome to us, as children. The annual market days, which occurred four times each year, were such events. On the day before these market days, traveling salespeople erected kiosks in the marketplace. On the day itself, the marketplace and the main streets were covered solidly with kiosks, open air sales tables, farmers' carts, and the like. These sales areas reached all the way to the livestock market. When the farmers were successful in getting good prices for their animals, they went to spend it on their own shopping. After the shopping, they went on to drink.

The special attractions for the children were the kiosks that offered gingerbread cookies. It was frustrating for us as children that we were usually short on cash and hence could seldom partake in all these wonderful offerings and then only to a limited extent. In the New Market there was usually also a carousel. This was of limited interest to me, as I only became dizzy when riding in the carousel. Sometimes there were also shows, but these were also not especially attractive to me. The main attraction for me was the high traffic level and the activity that took place along streets that normally were very quiet.

"Jacob" had his display of small goods that the farmers needed. These included everything from pocket knives to mirrors and from towels to handkerchiefs. I always admired the loud voice with which the salesmen announced the prices for their goods.

They started with a price that was three times their target price. They slowly lowered the price until they located a willing customer who was then followed by others, until they were often able to sell ten to twenty pieces of this item. Then they started the process all over again with a different sales item. I still remember the following saying that one of these sellers used: "Every spot and all dirt is removed by my brush, every louse, every bug runs away from this brush" [*this rhymes in German*]. This went on until late in the afternoon. By evening all was quiet again, and on the next day, the cleaning crew came and swept up the place.

This cleaning of the streets took place, at least during the summer months, every Wednesday and Saturday so that the streets were usually rather clean. The cleaning crew consisted of residents of the local prison, who had only one guard. The men wore prison garb while doing their work. I do not believe that any of them ever attempted to run away.

Another diversion was when the so-called Menagerie came traveling through Graetz. It usually consisted of a beat-up camel or dromedary, a few monkeys decorated with colorful rags, and one or two dancing bears. When we were very young, we enjoyed accompanying the Menagerie as it trekked through the town. As we got older, we just looked at the parade from the window of our house.

Twice a week, a group of traveling musicians was allowed to play on the town's streets. Usually, these were musicians playing on a lyre, but occasionally we also had musicians visit who played various wind instruments. Very rarely, a man came by who played four or even five different musical instruments all at one time, all by himself. On his head he would carry a tree of bells, and on his back was a kettledrum (which was belted together to one of his feet). He had a clapper tied to the other foot and usually he also played a carillon or a harmonica or some wind instrument. At other times a big wagon showed up, which was almost the size of a furniture movers' wagon. Inside the wagon was a lyre and the outer canvas was covered with drawings. These were usually horror scenes with numerous killings and blood streams. These wagons usually were led by a woman, who was equipped with a pointer. She sang songs about the depicted events and sold copies of her songs' texts. I have to admit that, as youngsters, these attractions terrified us and we stayed away from them.

Every year, we also had a school holiday, which was celebrated at the Gromblewoer Forest. In the early years, we traveled there in a wagon decorated in green colors. In later years, we traveled to this place by train. Out in the meadow, we participated in square dances, which we learned well in advance. We also participated in physical exercises, sang songs, and had some cakes, which were provided at a reasonable price by a local baker. Dinner was also provided, and, as night fell, we traveled back home on the last train of the day. From the train station in Graetz, we marched to the tunes of our musical band, while carrying lanterns. We walked to the town hall. On the way, residents of some of the houses sent up fireworks. At the town hall, one of the teachers or the District School Inspector would give a short speech, which no one could understand. We would salute the Kaiser and sing, with musical accompaniment, *"Heil Dir in Siegerkranz"* ["*hail to you who stands in the winner's circle*"]. With this the festival would come to an end.

Two or three times during my school days, the school put up theatrical performances to raise money for Christmas Charities, which were organized by the Fatherland's Women's Organization. I participated in two of these shows. The first one was called *Golden Marie and Bad Luck Marie*. I was still very young at that time and only played a minor role in that performance.

The second performance was of a play called *Lucky Child and Misfortune's Bird*. I was given one of the two leading roles. I played Misfortune's Bird. We had a lot of fun in both cases, especially when the rehearsals were taking place on the stage of a real theater. In the role of Misfortune's Bird, I was dressed in a borrowed black dancing dress. My mother had added white gauze frills and silver edgings. My hair was curled up to make it appear shorter. As a cover on my head, I wore a black Wagnerian cap, topped with some expensive white ostrich feathers. These feathers came from Mrs. Gruenberg, who made her whole household available on such occasions. I had a special success in this role, as many people who had known me on a daily basis did not recognize me in that role. We had a wonderful time while we were getting ready, and we were very proud that our effort generated generous gift-giving during the Christmas time.

Let me now mention the piano lessons I had with Mr. Viereck. This man was proud to his last days because he was the student of Loeschhorn, a well-regarded composer who had dedicated a study piece to him [*perhaps Carl Albert Loeschhorn*].

Other than that, we did our duty, sat during winter nights after dinner in the office and in the summer, on a bench in front of the entrance door to the house, or whatever we were otherwise inspired to do. The evening hours were the only time during the week when our mother was available for a relaxed conversation, except in cases where she was occupied in some other way by our father. Father was by nature very active and balanced. He seldom had the need for small talk. Although mother was stricter in many ways, father always kept a certain distance from us. Mother, in her humble way, could derive joy from looking at some green leaves or anything else that was pretty, especially from music. Under other circumstances, mother might have developed differently, but in her case, her talents remained uncultivated.

Although there were six of us siblings, we were seldom at home at one time. The elder sisters had to go to Posen or to Berlin to complete their education. For the brothers, the need to continue their education forced them to leave home early. This was the case because the plan to create an academic high school in town was voted down by the Cultural Ministry in spite of all the efforts of our father and our town's mayor. Mostly we were all together at home only during the school holidays, especially as Rosa got married early and only came to visit us on festive occasions. I was eleven years old when Rosa left my parent's house. We always understood each other well, considering our age difference. She had the most difficult task of all of us, in the rather large household. In spite of her relative weakness, she never complained or lost her cool. Bianka and I, on whose upbringing she spent much time, found her departure especially painful.

As a young child I found myself often alone amongst my siblings. Lenchen and Ernst on one side and Hugo and Bianka on the other were closer in age to each other. I was too young for the older kids and too old for the younger ones, which led me to shed tears, when I found myself as the one in between. That changed with time, as we grew older. With the exception of a short time, Ernst and I developed a very warm relationship. During the first school vacation, he developed a strong ego and every other word from him was, "I would be more qualified to understand this...." As I was about fifteen years old at that time and highly sensitive, this led to numerous fights between us. Later on, he was always very kind and brotherly to me. I must thank him for stimulating my interest in many things.

Hugo made use of the extended loutish years and knew how to get me mad at him. After he got me angry, when mealtime came and, in the absence of our mother who was away on her summer vacation, I was in charge, he would say, "At least during mealtime you do not let me feel your fury." He also got me mad at him when he referred to me by saying, "You, Hedelhedwig" [*it is unclear if this taunt had a meaning*]. I did not like my name enough to enjoy when it was abbreviated or modified. Basically, however, we were rather close. I had generally very good relations with Bianka, even though she sometimes was rather stubborn and, as the youngest child, got special treatment from our father. Later in life we became very good friends.

When my school days came to an end, so did my period as a young girl. My days as a maid started with the murky period of my late teen years. As I had already mentioned, I received further instruction a few hours each week from Miss Pohl and Dr. Lohrer. Dr. Lohrer received me always with a friendly greeting as "Miss Hedwig" and held my chair for me as a sign that I was no longer a school girl. In spite of this, the weeks felt endlessly long and too much time remained on my hands, without a satisfying purpose.

We had two helpers in the house who were rather good. Lenchen had overall responsibility for them, and she also supervised the activities of the dessert kitchen. That left for me only dusting and mending responsibilities. Had I been allowed to be lazy, I would not mind it, but Lenchen would not have any of it. So I spent all my time dusting and mending. There ensued many long and bitter fights, until I decided one day to end it all, with the aid of a bottle of bitter almond oil, which I thought would be the way to end this sad existence. I don't know whether or not I had already started taking the liquid when my Mother surprised me and was very kind to me. She gave me Baldrian drops to calm me down. She told me that the bitter almond oil would, at the most, have caused me to suffer from stomach troubles, as this liquid was of the strength prescribed as medicine for children.

Shortly after this, Lenchen went on a trip, which allowed me to participate in more of the household's activities. When she returned from her trip, she was in remarkably good spirits. A few days later two men, whom I did not know, came to visit from Stargard. One was an older gentleman by the name of Mr. Wedell. The other was a younger man, who was well dressed and wore a top hat and a fancy suit. He was introduced to us as the lawyer,

Mr. Meyer. This happened on May 24, 1893, the last day of Whitsun, when, as usual, Ernst was at home.

We had a nice lunch, a well-set coffee in the afternoon, and a special dinner. The conversation during these meals excluded us children. No one said anything or gave even a hint to what was going on. I did get the feeling, however, that something important was happening. It is claimed that I said to Bianka, as I was helping her get into her best dress, "Don't go outside the house, or people will think Lenchen is getting engaged." Normally, Ernst would have taken the evening train back to Posen. At my parents' urging, he remained at home until 10 p.m. in order to travel by cart to Opalenitza, so that he could carry with him the news, which Hugo and Rosa were awaiting.

Following dinner, my parents and Mr. Wedell went to a separate room. We were never told why their conversation was so lengthy. In any case, when Ernst entered their room to bid them farewell, at around 10, the final decision had not yet been reached. It was not until 10:30, when I was running up and down the stairs, that my mother called me so I could congratulate the lucky couple.

We children were curious to find out what our new brother-in-law's first name was. In his top hat we saw the letters "S. M." The new brother-in-law was a youthful man, who liked to tease the whole world and knew how to make a warm connection with everybody. After that, he came to visit frequently, and the wedding date was set for August. This resulted in a lot of preparation work in advance of the event for both Mother and Lenchen. It also gave me a freer hand. Even if I was sometimes inclined to get into mischief, the responsibility for cooking, baking, and shopping, at the age of fifteen, was the source of a lot of pleasure. I was no longer tired or strained.

At the special request of Samuel [*Lenchen's betrothed*], the wedding was to take place in Graetz. This resulted in much work for my mother. The immense heat that prevailed in August made things even more difficult, because almost all the food had to be brought from the outside. A cooking lady was summoned from Posen, with dishes and silverware. Much had to be stored and considered. The evening before the wedding was spent at home, while the wedding itself was planned for the community's social hall. This hall was especially suitable for the occasion, as it had a large shaded garden. It was a difficult problem to locate room to sleep all the guests who had come from out of town. We were able to accommodate several of the guests in our home. Others were placed in homes of various friends in town. For two or three days, we children were busy delivering cake to several of our guests, who were staying with friends. These days one can hardly imagine how much baking was involved in getting ready for such an affair.

On the day before the wedding, the civil marriage took place. In addition to Hugo and Rosa, Mama Minna Meyer, a very old but nice and smart woman, and a brother of Samuel were expected. The evening before the wedding was very nice. The old folks and the couple stayed in the so-called green room, the old "Good Room." The youngsters stayed in Lenchen's room, which was completely emptied for the occasion. There were plenty of younger people present. These included Samuel's younger brother Gustav, Adolfine Brodnitz, a nephew and niece of Samuel, Alfred Badt, Martha Badt, Hella Krombach, Ernst, and me. All of us were very exuberant, and we also danced.

The next morning, a goods wagon came from the brewery and picked up the cooking lady and all the accessories, serving dishes, etc., which were loaded onto it and transported to the hall. Some huge washing kettles loaded with ice were also brought there. At that point, the cooking and baking for the festivities got started.

The wedding itself took place in the hall, which was beautified by decorating the laurel trees around it. A big coffee table loaded with snacks was placed on the balcony of the garden. The youngsters ran around in the garden until it was meal time. Our family bore the bulk of the expenses that were incurred for this event. The guests appeared pleased, or at least pretended to be, and our family's various contributions and performances on that day drew much applause.

Hugo, Bianka, and I appeared dressed as a family of Gypsies, and we read a lengthy poem written by Aunt Mielziner. Hugo had the best part, as he represented the past and he could play tricks with great humor. Ernst and I performed next. We had a good time. Whether or not the viewers also enjoyed it, I would leave to others to say.

On the next day, the young couple left to start a wedding trip, which lasted six weeks. They were forced to stay away for so long because their apartment in Stargard became available only by October 1. I believe that they started their trip by going to Dresden and then on to Naples. On their way back, they also came for a short visit to our home.

By then the time had come for me to go to Berlin, to get my advanced schooling. I was supposed to go at the beginning of October to the pension of Mrs. Silbermann, where Rosa and Lenchen had already been before me. The purpose of this stay was to allow me to build up my limited skills in languages, music, and literature, as well as art history.

As my mother was tied up with work for the business, she could not take care of running the household at the same time. Therefore, at a time when no older daughter was available at home, she had to look for hired help. She found such a person in Miss Sara Flatau, the daughter of the caretaker of the Graetz Jewish Community, who wanted to work in our home. She was no longer very young or good looking, but, in her own way, she was rather efficient in housekeeping.

I left for Berlin in early October, on the first longer trip in which I had traveled alone. I was so excited that, unlike on other trips, I did not feel ill on the way. At the Alexanderplatz in Berlin I was greeted by Aunt Badt and Mrs. Silbermann who then accompanied me to Mrs. Silbermann's place at Magdeburger Street, No. 36. I arrived while the group was busy working with their hands. Sitting there was Trude Wedell (Samuel's niece, who had come to us for the wedding). She gave me a charitable look, the only one among the group of strangers. There were about twenty girls in the house, ranging in age from twelve to twenty years old. Most were, however, of roughly my age. I was assigned a small room that was shared with Trude Wedell and another young woman.

During the first evening, many of the usual dormitory tricks were played on me. There were peas under my bed sheet, a glove filled with wet sand was on my pillow case and baking powder was put in some household equipment. As I took it all well, I was accepted within a short time as a fellow student. We were all very friendly. Nonetheless, no lifelong friendships developed.

Silbermann was a hardworking and likable woman, whose luck in life underwent many fluctuations. She worked in the home of a man, who later became her husband, as a teacher for his daughters. After his first wife died, she married the man and they had a son and a daughter. They lived in Goerlitz in a wonderful house, and they had horses, etc.

Then the husband died, leaving her with five children and financial debts. This misfortune caused her to be somewhat bitter. She was clever enough to mask this bitterness while she was in the presence of the young ladies in her care. She was too full of spirit to be a very good educator. When she was in a good mood, she was very charming, but in insignificant matters, she was sometimes abrupt and unjust.

It must have been difficult to earn a living by taking care of young women at the most difficult part of their lives, especially as she had to start each year with a new group of residents. It was clearly a case where a lot of hard work was needed just to maintain order in such a house. On top of that, she tried to provide every girl with the desired classes, and she did so with the aid of just one helper.

Just providing food for such a group of girls was a challenge. The meals were somewhat simple, yet they were not bad. Every one enjoyed getting packages from home, but this was really not necessary. Some even got delicacies from home, which clearly was not necessary. Some of the girls purchased rolls with butter and sausages, which certainly were not needed, as one could always get enough food so that one never needed to go hungry. I was very thankful to my mother who had always insisted that I eat everything that was offered for a meal in our home. While I was not a big eater, I was usually the only one who ate everything. I rebelled once when we were given some burnt pea puree with sauerkraut for lunch. For the evening meal we were usually given cold cuts. The rule was that one should not place more than three pieces of the cold cuts on one piece of bread. Exceeding this count was considered greedy.

On Friday evenings, we were given fish with a mustard sauce. I enjoyed these dishes as a break from the weekly routine. These were the first fish from the sea that I had ever eaten [*all the others were, apparently, freshwater fish*]. Once every fourteen days we were given a special evening meal, which consisted of many saucers filled with herrings, salads, smoked meat, cheese, etc. We were given the freedom to put together whatever we wanted. In short, it was really not a difficult time.

From Monday through Friday, ten of us who were roughly the same age and who were no longer attending school, followed the same courses. An English lady lived in our house and ate with us. She gave us lessons in English, and in her free time she studied music. A French lady came each day and gave us lessons. Two teachers from a girl's school nearby came daily and gave us classes in literature and art history (both were rather dry and boring). We also had speech lessons twice a week, and every Wednesday from 10 a.m. until 1 p.m., we were taken by an elderly short lady, who was rather nearsighted, to visit a museum. She took us to the National Museum or to see modern or classic art, according to what the teacher had just discussed in class. Some of the girls were also given music lessons. On Saturday there were no classes, but Miss Beasley took us to visit other museums in the city, such as the Postal Museum, Smoking Museum, and Museum of the Kaiser's History, etc.

On Saturday afternoons, one could visit with relatives. Sunday was a free day, and during the summer months on Sunday afternoons, one could go out on the town. Soon, however, the dancing lessons started. These were scheduled for every Sunday afternoon from 5 to 7 p.m. We usually extended them until 8 or 9 in the evening. Mrs. Silbermann had put a lot of effort into these lessons. First the dining room had to be cleared, and the adjacent salon was also opened up. Mrs. S. saw to it that enough young men, some students, some businessmen, were present for the dance. She looked aside when a little flirtation took place. Our dancing teacher was a nice person who brought his piano player with him. When they left at seven o'clock, one of the students, usually Trude Sokolowski, who was very talented, played for the rest of us. Mrs. S. provided us with beer, carbonated water, and sometimes sandwiches. The freely arranged dancing gave us much pleasure.

Once or twice, we also had a coffee circle. The young ladies wrote some small theatrical acts that they then performed during those dancing lessons. Our wardrobe was very limited. At that time, I was certainly not spoiled. The only nice dress I owned was the one I got for Lenchen's wedding. It was a pink dress, made of crepe material, and it had white lace frills. I had to save this dress for the dancing ball! This was the big event for which we were preparing for weeks on end. The ball took place in a hall on Leipziger Street, where the Wertheim department store now stands. We were given coffee and cake and prepared a show for the "Gentlemen" in which I took part. The gentlemen also had surprise gifts for us, and we danced and danced until the early hours of the next morning. I don't believe that I have ever again danced as much as on that one occasion. It warmed my pride that I hardly ever had a chance to sit down. My cousin Bruno Mielziner, who was interested in one of the younger girls in our group, always made me aware of this fact. I had more fun on that night, without being romantically involved with anyone in the place. This ball marked the end of our dancing lessons. It remained, however, one of the nicest memories of my youth.

Mrs. Silbermann was very concerned about providing us entertainment. This was always done under the heading of "Education." Each week we attended a performance at the theater or a concert at least once. The Berlin Theater was a preferred destination. Barnay [*perhaps Ludwig Barnay*] was the director of this theater at that time, and he played in many of its key roles. We saw him perform in *Kean*, *Narzis*, *Wallenstein*, etc. He was especially good in his role in *The Priest from Kirchfeld*. Once we also went to the opera to see a performance of *Tannhauser*. We had tickets also for a performance of *Lohengrin*, which, at that time were very hard to get.

We lost our chance to go to hear this performance because of our stupidity. The English teacher wanted to dedicate all her time to her musical training. She was very nice to us and gave us some leeway during our after-the-meal walk. She did not pay attention when some of us stopped on the way to buy a slice of apple cake with whipped cream for 15 Pfennig(!). When she left, she was replaced by a nineteen-year-old woman who came to us directly from England. She was trying to cover her youth and inexperience by exerting her authority. She wanted us to walk on our hike in pairs. We asked Mrs. Silbermann to let us walk in a single line. We resented the young English teacher's attempt at forcing us to follow her line. During one of her English classes, one of us sat down at her desk. Only after she repeated several times, "I must sit on the top of my desk" was the place vacated. We discovered that the poor thing had put paper in the ball of her hair, which made her head look larger. She also wore clothes of unusual designs and funny hats.

One day during our English class, the five of us who were in attendance performed passive resistance. While some were reading German books, I strolled through the room and Trude Wedell stood behind her back and pointed to the paper in her hair. At that point Mrs. S. walked into the classroom, and all hell broke loose. We were informed at that point that the tickets to the opera performance of that night had already been picked up. As punishment for our behavior, Mrs. S. saw to it that the tickets were given back to the theater. Mrs. S. did, however, recognize that the teacher was not appropriate for our group. She obtained the services of an older and wiser lady, who came to our place for a few hours at a time. Of all the concerts, those performed by the Philharmonic Orchestra were the ones we preferred. They were more appropriate for people of our age and circumstances. They also had the advantage of being more reasonably priced.

Already on the third day of my stay in Berlin, during my first visit to Aunt Stern, I received a ticket to a performance of the Ninth Symphony [*possibly Beethoven*] as a gift from her son. I am not sure that I did get the full value of the performance at that time, but it filled me completely to my innermost self. Our many cousins from the Stern and Badt families were especially nice to me. When I came to visit their parents on a Sunday afternoon, they took me for a walk in Charlottenhof and other such places. Benno Stern was especially nice to me. Whereas the other nephews took the attitude of an older uncle toward me, he treated me like an adult. The uncles and aunts were always friendly, but they were surely annoyed when I was not warmer. Aunt Mielziner made an effort to get a bit closer to me. This was in spite of the fact that her financial circumstances were the most restricted and she was running a difficult household with four young children. She had rented a very modest place at Friedrichshagen for the summer months and insisted that I come to visit her on Saturday and Sunday. I finally took her up on this offer and went to her place with Benno Stern.

We met on a Sunday morning at the urban railroad station from where we traveled together. For the first time, I saw some of the areas that surround Berlin. I found the Mueggelsee to be especially nice. In the afternoon, we took a ride on a steamer, together with the Mielziner family. In the course of this trip, a storm broke out and we all ended up drenched. In the apartment of my aunt, we were lent some clothing to change into. As the aunt was significantly bigger and fuller than I was and the uncle smaller and skinnier than my cousin, one can imagine what a jolly appearance we must have made. After dinner, my cousin returned to the city, while I stayed until the next morning. At that point, I had to put on the dress, which looked dreary, and the new summer jacket that was not waterproof and that showed spots wherever rain drops had hit it. My uncle suggested a tailor, whom I visited on the way home, who was able to repair the damage.

A short time after this day, Mrs. S. took us for a day trip. We traveled by train to Neubabelberg, and, as I seem to remember, we continued from there by steamboat over the Griebnitzsee to a park and a castle. After viewing the castle and the park, we traveled by horse-drawn coach to Glienicker Brueke and on to Potsdam.

Actually, we went to Sanssouci. At that place, we visited the castle, the picture gallery, the Orangerieschloss, the park, and whatever else there was to see. This was, of course, a very hectic day, but that was part of Mrs. Silbermann's proven system. We ended the tour at the Wildpark station, which was just being locked up because the Kaiser and his wife were expected to arrive.

This addition to the plan allowed us to see the Kaiser in person for the first time, but it left us rather cool. That was not surprising as, at home, I had frequently heard critical remarks about the Kaiser's erratic behavior and lack of superiority and about his exaggerated pride and his tendency to be an absolute ruler of the country. Even after he governed just a few years, he had made himself rather unpopular. Father, in his function as chairperson of the local council, had to attend a special annual meal celebrating the Kaiser's birthday. Each time, he made it clear before or after that event that he was glad it was over. My parents' skeptical views, and their attitude that we saw at home toward the Prussian-German monarchy, were probably the source of my longstanding republican point of view.

We had dinner at the Wildpark train station. This is significant in that I took a chance for the first time and ordered a cutlet (i.e., *treif* [*nonkosher*]!). Mrs. Silbermann shook her head but let me do it. At the time, the whole trip appeared to me to have been wonderful. Only later did it become clear to me how silly this act of mine was.

For the half-year period that began in the summer, our schedule became less rigid because the dancing classes and the frequent visits to the theater or to concerts had come to an end. During the holidays, in October, I was at home for ten days as we celebrated Hugo's bar mitzvah. Hugo had left our parents' home at an earlier age than I did. He was a real failure at school and, with a heavy heart, our parents gave up after all the possibilities of teaching him in Graetz had been exhausted. They thought that they were doing the right thing when, on the advice of Grandmother Badt, they sent him to a teacher by the name of Jacobsohn, who taught only three or four young fellows.

Mr. J. was a very religious man, but not much of an educator. His wife was not very bright and not a loveable person. Both were clearly not the right people to care for and bring up a difficult young man, as Hugo was at that time. The meals were rather good at their place, but very fatty. As a result of this, within one year on this diet and without much physical activity, the skinny fellow who was constantly in motion, turned into a small fatty fellow. I received a scare when I saw Hugo after he had been there for half a year. Mr. J. had prepared Hugo for his bar mitzvah, and he sat with satisfied pride when his pupil raced, without making a mistake, through his *Maftir* portion.

During the days after the celebration, all of the children (of whom there were eight, including Hugo and Samuel) and several uncles and aunts came to our home. I used this opportunity to ask my parents' permission to allow me to do something that was dear to my heart. I wanted to take lessons in tailoring and in millinery, as I felt, already at that time, that such practical skills would be of great help in the future. I actually never discovered what had caused my father to object to this idea. It is possible that his feeling about being above the riffraff caused him to feel that his daughter should not learn such plain skills. He absolutely did not want to consider this proposal. I did not get a direct rejection of my suggestion but, when I continued to press him in letters from Berlin, he suggested that, if I desired, I might take a course in using the typewriting machine at Lettehaus. I was told that he was considering the purchase of a typewriter for the business, which was supposed to give me the incentive to start this training. I completed the training so that at its end, I was able to type rather well and fast. As it turned out, no such machine was ever purchased by the business, so this effort was rather wasted. I have regretted that I did not simply take the tailoring course, without informing my parents.

A minor misdeed, which could have resulted in a major problem, took place on a Sunday of that period. We were not invited to go out and we were sitting on the balcony of the house, while Mrs. S., her daughter, and Miss Wohl, were away. We suddenly had the idea that we would like to hire a coach with two horses and go for a ride. This by itself might have been a minor violation had we decided to take a ride at the zoo. However, we instructed the coachman to take us to the area of the Linden where a whole lot of other coaches were riding. I do not know how the others in our group felt, but I was afraid we might be seen by someone who knew us. I was relieved when we returned to our place without being seen.

Finally the first of July came, and with it ended the wonderful time in Berlin, and I had to return to my home. For a long time after it ended, the period I had spent in Berlin with all its pleasures stayed with me as a pleasant memory. For the first time in my life, I had so-called girlfriends, and that brought with it much enjoyment. I do not believe that my time in Berlin had a significant effect on my spiritual development. I was probably too young to be changed by what I got to see and to hear.

Basically, I just got a further education. I did gain some real skill with the English and French languages, which, unfortunately, I lost in future years by lack of practice. My feeling at that time that I was rather educated is perhaps not surprising, considering the background of most of the people at my hometown with whom I had contact upon returning from Berlin. Only at a later date did I strike up a friendship with Frieda Jablonski, who was the daughter of a classmate of my father. She was a rather nice friend who had spent a year in Heidelberg where she got a broader education. We could, therefore, talk about many things about which the other young ladies in town had no idea. She got married a year before I did and had some misfortune.

Before we, the so-called sisters in the boarding house, went on our Easter break, we bought each other a small golden chain with a small heart, to mark our commitment to a long-lasting friendship. I had the misfortune to have lost my chain while I was at home. I took it off before taking a bath and forgot to put it on again afterward. I didn't notice this oversight until the following day. Finding the chain missing, I suspected our maid, but the chain never turned up again. A few weeks after this event, when Father visited me in Berlin, he brought the chain. He told the dramatic tale about how the maid I'd suspected had stolen it and then lied. She was, of course, suspended from her duties at once.

The disappearance of the chain had some unexpected bad consequences. Mother declared that the household did not require four helpers anymore. As I was returning home soon, and as the other maid was relieved, Mother would reorganize the household. One maid would do the heavy work and the other maid and I would cook for the family on alternate weeks. I was not happy about this news nor about the fact that, unlike Rose and Lenchen who got a room for themselves when they returned home, I was asked to share a room with Bianka. This was understandable from a strictly logical point of view, but was not in line with my expectation to finally have a room for myself. Sharing the room also caused some tension between Bianka and me. I had often expressed my dissatisfaction about this arrangement, and I suspect that Bianka was correct in many such events. Other than that, Bianka and I got along very well, and once I got married, Bianka was always happy to come and visit us.

My relationship with the household helper was also somewhat strained. She was about ten years older than I, and she had a rather high idea of her value, despite having only a very limited education.

The shared kitchen duties were also a bit of a chore, because the only maid who was left in the household was kept busy cleaning the various rooms of the house. As a result, she was not available to help with cleaning vegetables, peeling potatoes, fetching coal or water for the kitchen, and similar tasks. In other words, the work entailed not just cooking the meals, but also all the other unpleasant jobs related to cooking. I handled these tasks for two years, on alternate weeks. Then one day I declared to my Mother: "I have by now mastered the needed cooking skills. From now on, Miss Flatau can take over the daily cooking, while I'll help in keeping the rooms clean and with the sewing. I'll also keep the responsibility for cooking specialty items and for the baking." Mother agreed to this suggestion. According to my father, I was very good at cooking fish, which we had every Friday evening. When I came back home from a trip and resumed cooking the fish, my father would exclaim, "It is obvious that Hedwig has cooked our fish dish." This caused some bad feeling on the part of Miss Flatau but gave me much pleasure, as I was not spoiled through frequent compliments by my parents. Miss Flatau was much better than I at doing the shopping for the house.

Upon returning home from the stay in Berlin, I was given at once, without a break or an adjustment period, the daily chores. Considering that I had poor blood and frequent headaches, it was not always easy to carry out my duties. I did often complain to myself that I had to be responsible for so much work around the house. In later days, I frequently thanked my mother for instilling in me the feeling of complete independence and a sense of freedom from others, when I was maintaining my own household. She herself was accustomed to depend on her own abilities and made demands on herself, in spite of her body's weakness and her frequent illnesses. She, therefore, expected the same from her children. It would have been nice had they occasionally tried to

Young Hedwig back in Graetz, Posen, in the 1890s

correct the blood condition with something other than the hated "Lewico-Water." Then again, I have been lucky, at least so far, and I have been able to keep up, at least as well as most others, who were protected and cared for whenever they were in pain. One of the advantages for me from having Miss Flatau in our home was that it made it easier for me to get time off for traveling. Although my mother did not like me to go away for longer periods of time, she was agreeable to more frequent short trips to Posen.

Shortly after my return home from Berlin, Mother left for her regular trip to the health baths in Karlsbad. A short time after her return, on September 4, my eldest nephew was born in Stargard. I was happy and proud to have become an aunt. Mother left at once to help Lenchen in Stargard, and she stayed there for about three weeks, to support Lenchen. I was certainly too young to have been of much assistance to Lenchen. The little baby was the first one I had viewed from nearby, and I found him lovely.

Near the end of my visit, the social club, of which Samuel [*Meyer, Lenchen's husband*] was the president, had a festive evening, in which some dancing took place. I stayed in Stargard over the Jewish New Year's Day and Yom Kippur. I missed being in my parents' home for Yom Kippur, as this day began in our home in a special way. Before sunset on the Eve, we ate a large meal that included a beef soup, chicken, and stewed fruit. The chicken was a so-called Kippur Chicken. On the day before the *Erev* Yom Kippur [*the evening before the holiday*], each member of the family was given a live chicken (for the women) or a hen (for the men) with its legs tied together. While saying certain blessings, the animal was swung overhead three times, something that I detested and which I was glad to miss. These animals were supposed to take upon themselves the sins of the person. They were killed shortly after the ceremony. This might have made sense had the chicken then been given to the poor to eat. It was, however, the tradition that the chickens were consumed during the meal that was eaten just before or just after fasting for Yom Kippur.

On the day before Yom Kippur, the children were sent to visit the home of some poor people, to give them gifts. There were numerous poor who did not want to get these presents. One pretended to come for a visit and just left the money in their places. I must confess that I, for one, was always glad when this tour, which took place during all the Jewish holidays, was behind me. Few of the poor in our town lived in clean and airy places. Most recipients accepted the gifts as if it was their right to get them, while others addressed one with excessive sweetness. It is hard for me to say which approach was harder to take. Each of the girls in the family was also obliged to make these rounds with bigger amounts of money, a short time before our wedding day. From early childhood it was impressed on us that each of us had a religious obligation to do good deeds and help the poor. My grandfather believed one had to be thankful to the poor if one was better off, and that, according to Jewish Law, one had the obligation to give 10 percent of one's income to the poor.

After the significant meal on Yom Kippur Eve, we lit major lights that were to last for twenty-four hours, and then all of us went to the synagogue to listen to the *Kol Nidre* service. This, I must confess, was the only service in the Graetz congregation that truly impressed me. The service was in the strictly orthodox tradition. All prayers were said in Hebrew, without the accompaniment of a choir or an organ.

A few reform steps that my father, who was rather conservative, supported were introduced into the service, but only following a major effort. There was, for example, the tradition that on certain days the *Cohanim* or *Levis*, that is, those who were descendants of the families that used to serve in the Temple in Jerusalem, would bless the congregation from the altar of the synagogue. As the number of those who could function in that role had shrunk, and the two or three who remained were no big lights in daily life, my father got together with the rabbi at that time, a Dr. Friedmann, who was a nice person and not a religious zealot, and they agreed that the rabbi would give the blessing to the congregation. The "Rabble," as my father used to call them, were not happy with this change, but they had to accept this new way. A Rabbi Dr. Silberberg, who came at a later day, wanted to revert to the former, traditional way, but to no avail.

In his speeches to the congregation, Dr. Friedmann did not just quote old sayings but was very nice to listen to. My sisters and I went to the synagogue only on holidays. After the *Kol Nidre* service, which was at least two hours long, we went back home, and soon thereafter we went to sleep. Some members of the congregation spent the whole night at the synagogue. This caused some Christians to refer to Yom Kippur as "The Long Night." My parents got up early to go to services and were away from the house when we got up on the following morning. Father stayed in the synagogue for the entire day, while Mother would come home in midday and rest a bit in the sofa bed. The older men dressed in a long white shirt over their suits and a simple white head cover with some embroidery. They also wore a prayer shawl and instead of regular shoes, they wore slippers. The older women, not including my mother, wore special white dresses, a large sheet of clothing, which traditionally was given to each bride by her groom, and slippers.

The poor Rabbi had to give two sermons on Yom Kippur, one during the morning and another during the evening services, so, in addition to having had to fast the whole day, he had to achieve this too. Personally, I attended only the morning services, because, while the fasting per se was not a problem for me, I usually developed a bad headache, which allowed me to miss the evening service. This was good, as the air in the synagogue was rather foul by that time of the day.

During one year when the weather was especially warm during the holidays, several cases of cholera occurred. The police came and insisted that the temple be vacated for an hour to allow the place to get aired out. This triggered some changes in the air handling system so that the problem of an interrupted service did not reoccur.

As children, we were not expected to fast the whole day until we reached our twelfth birthday. We, however, tried to fast even at a younger age. I believe that our parents looked kindly at our attempts to fast at a younger age. In spite of her severe illness during her last years, Mother continued to fast on the holiday until her death. For the older generation, fasting was not just an obligation or a tradition. It also was a way of communicating with God on that day. This resulted in a very tender atmosphere in my parents' house at the closing of this holiday. Father, who was usually very reserved, kissed each of us with tears in his eyes at the meal at the end of the holiday, after the famous three stars were seen in the evening sky.

The meal was started by having sweet fried rings [*possibly doughnuts*], which were reputed to regenerate the stomach juices. These were followed by coffee and cake. Our brothers did not seem to need anything to get their juices flowing, as they caused a mountain of cake to disappear. The surprising thing is that this almost never led to an upset stomach. One hour after this, the evening meal was served. This one was similar to the one that we had on the night before the fasting had begun. With this meal, the day came to an end and everyone was pleased to have it behind them for another year.

My grandfather observed also other holidays, such as the ninth day of the month of *Av*, the day that the Temple in Jerusalem was destroyed (by the Romans in the year A.D. 72). He also observed the fasting day in remembrance of *Gedaljah*. At our home, this day was observed by eating only dairy items during our midday meal, which was actually seen by us children as a celebration.

Coming back to my tale: In Stargard, Yom Kippur took a different appearance. I was the only one who fasted. Samuel went to the synagogue in the morning. The whole day seemed just like an obligation that one had to do for God, but nothing else.

After three weeks had passed, I returned to our home. A very quiet winter followed, during which I had much free time and leisure time to contemplate the nice winter months of the previous year and I had time to read and study languages. I would have made poor choices in selecting my reading material had my brother Ernst not helped me a bit in getting worthy books.

A short time after my return from Stargard, our family physician and his wife celebrated their silver wedding anniversary. My parents were invited for a dinner at their place and went during the morning to the couple's house to offer their best wishes. I was rather surprised when, suddenly, Mrs. Robinson urged my mother to bring me along for dinner. In the evening, a man who was no longer very young, a bit short and stout, who was the brother of the lady of the house, was assigned to be my tablemate. He was not exactly a great companion, but he did not leave my side.

On the following day, a charity performance took place at my former school. My sister Bianka and the youngest daughter of the Robinsons took part in this performance. The smallish fat man also was there, again. As I was to learn only later, he took a liking to me when I was only sixteen years old. Twice he had sent his sister to my parents, asking for their permission to become their son-in-law. The first time they were approached, my mother used the excuse that at sixteen, I was too young to be considered ready for such a step. The second time he approached them, the situation was more difficult as I was by then eighteen years old. My father felt obliged to examine the situation carefully.

My mother was at that time on a trip to Posen, Stargard, and Berlin and discussed the situation with Hugo, Samuel, and Uncle Louis Badt. She got feedback about the candidate that was not favorable. They could have spared themselves this effort had they talked to me about this idea. When I heard, much later, that this small fat man was supposed to be my husband, I broke out laughing. My parents had the opinion, however, that the parents must do their examination of the candidate before consulting with their daughter. However, they would never have forced such a "candidate" on their daughters. Life was made easy for my parents when their younger two daughters left their supervision.

In my rather steady life, the short and longer trips became the most pleasant breaks. Each year I went for a couple of weeks to Stargard and, more frequently, on shorter trips to Posen. We also went occasionally to Posen to purchase toiletry items for the house. Once, on such a trip, I was allowed to stay a bit longer in Posen.

The visits to Posen and Stargard represented rather different events. In Posen, there was a comfortable atmosphere. Much attention was placed on good food and delicacies, which the small household could afford better than our large family at home.

Hugo and Rosa often took me to the theater, and I was able to listen to many good concerts and lectures. I was allowed to sleep until late, which always made it a very nice visit for me. What was missing there, which I found in Stargard, was sociability. Since the death of Mama Brodnitz and even more so, after the father died, a short time before my eighteenth birthday, the family in Posen lived a very withdrawn existence.

In Stargard, on the other hand, theater and other entertainment were lacking. There was much more socializing there, and each year they celebrated a major feast. This involved performances with music and dancing, and I always had a great time. Lenchen in her kindness made sure to always invite me in time for the feast. Only once did my parents agree to come with me to the festival in Posen. They made the sacrifice, and such it was for them because the trip and the long and active night were done only to give me pleasure. We had a very boring companion at our table, and although I had danced a lot on that occasion, the attempt to humor me was not a real success and was never repeated again by my parents.

One of the attractions of visiting Stargard was that I had a nephew there. He was the only nephew at that time and was a lovely youngster. After a lengthy struggle, I was able to get permission to accept an invitation to visit our relatives in Glogau. The household of my uncle and aunt Badt was not maintained as a "kosher" place. This caused serious pain to my grandmother Badt, who was still alive at that time. Grandmother had a hard time in accepting that first Lenchen and later I were allowed by our mother to visit there, as this gave official sanction to our eating *treif* food. Life in Glogau was very enjoyable. The aunt was a very happy youthful woman, the uncle was constantly teasing, and the three girls were very jolly. As a result, one could satisfy one's appetite just from all the ongoing laughter.

The middle daughter, named Else, was very dear to me. I was not allowed to show this affection, as the eldest girl, Martha, would have been jealous. When I visited there and when they came to visit us, we were inseparable. None of us were very good at writing letters. Even birthday letters were limited to the shortest possible form. I gave them a gift of a rubber stamp that stated, "Best wishes from Martha, greetings from Else and also Grete," which they subsequently used when sending greetings. We had a circle of eight to ten young girls. We made each other the promise never to get married. Should one of us decide to break this promise, her bridegroom would be required to get the others' release from this promise by giving all the others a big amount of chocolate as compensation. I was the first one to get married, and my husband-to-be fulfilled his obligation in a most noble manner.

During my second visit to Glogau, I learned, together with my cousins, how to ride a bike. It happened as follows: A courageous master locksmith, who owned a ladies' bike, came with one of his assistants to our street. He took us in turns to learn to ride the bike. He first taught us how to use the foot brakes. He next brought his own bike and tied it to the student's bike. In this manner we went off riding. It went well, but occasionally we also took a spill. We learned to ride the bike within a rather short time. On coming back from such a learning trip, my youngest cousin, Grete, informed us with a big smile that she had learned that the bike was only three years younger than she was, or fourteen years old. That was how it actually looked. We did, however, gain a lot of reasons to laugh from these lessons.

Glogau is located in a very nice area. Every Sunday we took lovely rides in my uncle's buggy and we swam in the cold water of the River Oder. As, unfortunately, I could only stay there for brief periods, I did not learn how to swim. I was very jealous of Else, who was very good at it.

I had timed my visits to Glogau so that I would be home during school breaks. This way, I was back at home when Ernst came back home. His return always made the place much livelier. In 1896, I gave up a chance to visit Berlin and attend a trade show in order to be able to go to visit in Glogau. I went back to Berlin during the winter of 1897, but it was not a pleasure trip. My aunt Mielziner became seriously ill with a case of jaundice and required the help of a nurse for weeks on end. I don't know whether or not our relatives in Berlin had requested my help or whether it was my mother's idea. All I know is that my Grandmother was very unhappy that I was asked to help in order to save money on a nurse. Mother had, however, accepted the request and did not want to go back on her word.

The three weeks in Berlin turned out to be very difficult and required much effort. There was only one maid in the house, and she was not very capable. The aunt also required a special diet. On top of this, the uncle and the three children, two of whom were already working in the business, had completely different meal times. The aunt was expected to be taken for a walk at midday. She needed much help in this endeavor. In short, it was not easy to fulfill all their expectations. The only comfort for me was the youngest daughter by the name of Lucie. Lucie died a few years after my stay, but she was never really healthy. She was a dear child.

The other relatives who were living in Berlin at that time tried to make up for my difficult time by inviting me for dinner or by taking me to the theater. Even Aunt Badt came forth with an invitation to the theater. The best performance at the opera was when I went to see *Freischuetz* with Benno Stern. Thanks to his position on the stock exchange, Benno was able to get us tickets for excellent seats. I also got to see a performance of *Carmen* with Lenchen and Samuel, who came to Berlin for a few days.

For Christmas Eve, I was invited to visit Albert Stern, who had gotten married a short time before that day. The wife was so kind to me that I could hardly believe it when I learned later that she was very difficult with Albert. They got divorced after a while. At a later date, I found out why the wife was so nice to me. Luckily, I was completely unaware that various family members were making an effort to get me to side with them.

Thanks to Hugo Brodnitz and his sensitive and clever nature, I was spared some attempts by family members to get me matched up with some of their friends or relatives. He informed my parents about these ideas, and they, in turn, put an end to it, saving me from the need to fight such approaches.

These theatrical shows were very nice, but it was hard to get up early the next morning and carry out one's duties. As a result, when I returned home on New Year's Eve, I was rather weak and run down. Luckily, the Eve passed in our home in an uneventful way, which I welcomed. We did have punch and pancakes for supper, but my parents went to sleep at 11 p.m., and so did the children. I slept until late into New Year's Day, without even guessing what changes the New Year would bring for me!

Our grandmother, who was eighty-four years old and had been still active in the household of Aunt Krombach, suddenly became seriously ill. My mother went to visit her regularly and sometimes spent a few days with her. Finally, on the evening before Lag BaOmer, Grandmother drifted into a final sleep with the prayer *"Shma Israel"* on her lips. In all our sadness, I could but smile when it was learned that Grandmother passed away five minutes before the arrival of Shabbat. According to Orthodox Jewish traditions, had she died five minutes later, we could never visit her burial place! This death time was established by Uncle Krombach, who was an especially observant Jew. Uncle Krombach was only in his forties at that time, but this once-strong man was already suffering awful pains caused by his illness.

Frequently when Mother returned from her visits to Posen, she said that Hugo Brodnitz had requested, "Please send Hedwig to visit us." In my pride, I declared that only if both Hugo and Rosa invited me would I go.

As a reward for her good marks at school, Bianka was allowed to travel to Posen for Whitsunday, while my parents were going for a visit in Stargard. This was the first time that both could travel together in peace, as Father had just sold the retail store on the first of April. Following the sale, we all moved to the upper floor of our building, while the new buyer took over the sales area and all the rooms on the ground floor, which became his dwelling place. This was not an easy move for my parents.

Mother had long been suffering from extensive pain, and my parents had consulted Professor Gerhard in Berlin, who suggested that, for the sake of my mother's health, they had to give up the business. Father retained the brick factory and several parcels of real estate that he was developing. He made an office for himself in the former storage rooms. We had enough furniture in the house to furnish the office. It was very pleasant to stay in the office during the summer months. During the winter, however, it was impossible to get the office to be comfortable, even while using the heater that was in that room. The same was true for my parents' bedroom, which was located just above the office. Previously they were able to move during the colder months to a warmer room. Now, however, the house was smaller and no other room was available. This continually cold room was not what Mother needed in her weakened condition. These moves, and all the effort they entailed, fortunately occurred before Grandmother became ill.

My parents were getting ready for a leisurely trip to Stargard, while I was looking forward to having a relaxed time alone in the house. Suddenly I received a very warm invitation from Rosa, whereupon the four of us traveled to Posen instead of going to

Stargard, on Friday before Whitsun. My parents continued at once on their way to Stargard, to avoid traveling on Shabbat.

In Posen, I was surprised to learn that Julius Brodnitz was expected to come for a visit on the following day. Wonderful days followed. Rosa was especially cooperative and willing to partake in all activities. I could not believe my ears when Julius suggested on the following Friday that we take a morning walk in the local zoo, including a breakfast at that park. Rosa agreed to it at once. When he appeared in the morning to pick us up, he brought with him roses for the three of us [*Rosa, Bianka, and Hedwig*] but he had two dark red roses, only for me. My heart started pounding with excitement. I thought that I was only a fool and that it was just a coincidence. We stayed together the whole time and talked about God and the world. It is said that I made some stupid remarks about marriage so that it must have taken some real courage for him to want to have me as a wife. I was needled about this endlessly, especially when the reality turned out so different from my theories.

The beautiful day came to an end, and I traveled back home with my mother, who had returned from Stargard. She got severe pain in her back during the trip and had to rest in bed as soon as we reached home. I sat by her bed doing some mending, and we talked. Since she was no longer involved in the business at this time, she now had more free time and she enjoyed talking to me. One day a young lady in the circle of our friends got engaged to be married. It followed the description: "He came, he saw, and he conquered." The candidate came for coffee, and the friends were already invited by whispered invitations. I stated that I would never agree to get married in such a rushed way. Mother said she thought if the parents were convinced it was in my best interest, I should let them make the decision for me. On this opportunity, my mother told me about the various offers they'd had for my hand, some direct and others roundabout, which they had refused. I was amused and perhaps a bit proud, but I said to her that I would rather stay single than agree to such an "arranged" marriage.

The following Sunday, we celebrated my father's sixtieth birthday. This was the first time we celebrated his birthday according to the German calendar. The children and children-in-law were all there to have pictures taken. Hugo, Rosa, Lenchen with Kurt [*her son, Kurt Meyer*], and Hugo Herzfeld were there. Ernst could not come as he was serving his year of military service in the Artillery and was away from Posen in field test firing. Samuel could only come late, and we celebrated the birthday in a small family circle. As was customary for him, Hugo Brodnitz went back to Posen on that evening. Rosa stayed behind until Monday night. At that point Lenchen and Kurt, who was loved by all and whom we enjoyed spoiling, were alone with us.

On Wednesday morning, we got a dispatch from Rosa saying she would be coming for a visit that afternoon. When she arrived, she explained her sudden visit by saying that her husband had suddenly been forced to go alone on a business trip.

After the evening meal, she pulled me aside to one of the bedrooms and gave me a letter to read. The letter was addressed to her but one look at it changed my whole life. Without a moment's hesitation, I responded to the question in the letter with a clear "Yes." Not recklessly but having my dreams fulfilled, I was very clear in my wishes, so I did not need even a second to think it through. Possibly, I was a bit confused, but certainly very happy, when I went to Mother, who shared my happiness. As happened frequently, Father was on a business trip. He was on a longer stay in Dortmund as a delegate to a convention of the tile producers' association.

Rosa went back home on that evening. Before she left, we agreed that we would get engaged at her place, where we had found each other. She was most outgoing to us and assured us later that our engagement was the best birthday gift she had ever received. The few days left until Julius' arrival on Saturday, June 11, 1898, passed in exciting and restless anticipation. I was concerned not about my luck, but about his. I was, however, too young to dwell on such concerns. We needed only a few words and a short time until we gave each other our hands. I will thank my luck until the end of my days that it led me in that direction.

As our engagement came on the heels of several painful events that had befallen the Brodnitz family, the joy of the event was multiplied manyfold. Julius' siblings welcomed me with a warm heart. As we all had known one another for a long period before the event, it did not take long for us to become close friends. I also received such very warm letters from his friends that I was almost embarrassed.

We got engaged on the next day, at my parents' place. We obtained the blessings of my parents in part from Graetz and in part by telegram from Dortmund. As the second one had to be delivered by hand and took a while to be delivered, Julius teased me the whole day long that I could still change my mind, as we only had half the blessing.

We celebrated our engagement with our Hugo, Rosa and Hugo Herzfeld, as well as Alfons and Bertchen, Aunt Krombach, and Martin, who was representing the Berlin branch of the family. Samuel also was there. On the other hand, Ernst and Hermann were both in Hammerstein for field training and could not come.

Father managed to return home in time. Both of my parents, especially Mother, welcomed Julius as if he had been their own son. On Monday afternoon, Julius had to depart. He promised me that he would be back for my birthday on June 22, in spite of the fact that, with his busy schedule, it was not easy for him to take time out in the middle of the week. He arrived, and we spent the day with only our closest circle and without any outsiders. On the other hand, letters and best wishes kept pouring in. It felt rather strange for me to be the central object of so much love and friendship.

Draft copy of the invitation to Hedwig and Julius' wedding in 1898

On that day it was also agreed that I would travel with my parents to Landeck at the beginning of the month of July. Julius was going to join us for three weeks, as soon as the court's summer holidays got started. We looked forward with pleasure to that time. All was arranged for that trip. Bianka was going to visit relatives, and, for the first time in my parents' long marriage, the house would be locked up and empty. One night, just before our departure, Mother suffered from a sudden drop in her blood pressure, so it was not possible for her to travel. We were very concerned about her condition, but thanks to her resilience and will power, she was able to go to Reichenhall in order to part take in a *Kur* [*a health treatment*].

The trip was rather difficult. We had to travel fifteen hours to Vienna. There we stayed overnight. The next day we traveled during most of the day until we reached Reichenhall. Our weak mother withstood the trip better than I did. I was half dead by the time we got to Reichenhall. The first few days were a washout because of rain. Our suitcases were late to arrive by several days. Moreover, as I had not received any mail from Berlin [*Julius*], I was in a bad mood.

At long last the weather improved, and then Julius joined us. These three weeks in Reichenhall were the best period of our engagement. We could not have wished for ourselves anything better and more beautiful than being in a wonderful location without having to worry about obligations to family or friends. The three of us or all four went also on wonderful trips to Salzburg, Berchtesgaden, and Koenigsee. The most wonderful time was when we went walking hand in hand on a beautiful path, without having to pay any attention to the passing time. Mother was more understanding than my father and let us have more free time. As my parents knew several of the visitors at the spa, they were not dependent on us for company.

While at Reichenhall, I got to know Benno and Alice Braun and the parents and the sister of Ernst Kirsch. Father had no patience to stay there for the duration. During the last eight or ten days, we remained in the place, only with my mother. For a while, we were also visited by Hugo and Rosa as well as by Samuel and Lenchen. Julius also had to leave us toward the end of the stay, so Mother and I were the last of our small group to leave.

We traveled back again through Vienna where we had planned to stay for a couple of days to take in the sights of that beautiful city. However, it rained with such violence that we did not get to see anything of its beauty. Mother did not want to go to the theater as she was still in mourning, and the museums were closed during our stay. The visit was really a waste of time. We, therefore, continued our travels earlier than we had planned. On our way back, we made a short stop at the home of Ferdinand Landsberg, who lived in Brieg. He was a cousin of my parents, and they welcomed us warmly and asked us to stay a bit longer. We traveled on that evening and after a short stay in Breslau, we continued on to our home.

After that, I went frequently to Posen to purchase my trousseau. In Posen, a painful event took place within the family circle. Uncle Krombach's sickness was progressing rapidly, and it became clear after a short time that he could not be saved. This sad realization of my uncle's impending death cast a shadow on all of us.

Twice we had the pleasure of having Julius come to us for a visit. The third planned visit did not take place as planned. Uncle Krombach underwent a surgery in early October that saved him from further suffering. Instead of coming to visit, Julius came with us to the funeral.

On October 26, 1898, Julius took me from my parents' home. With full trust and confidence, we walked toward our new life together!

With this I would like to close the memories of my youthful years. My parents tried, in their own way, to provide for us a trouble-free youth. They attempted to bring us up as useful people. Even if the way they selected for us was not always the one we wanted to follow (and which older generation does not experience this with the next generation?), I am still thankful for their efforts. I was able to grow up in an atmosphere that was always pure, and I must thank them for what I have become. Without this foundation, even my best educator, who is still taking me to school every once in a while, and who, I hope, will continue to do so for a long time to come, would not have been able to achieve what he has. If my children remember their parents' home in the same way I remember mine, then I will have achieved a lot.

[*This addition was written by Hedwig in the summer of 1931.*] When I read these notes now, eight years after they were first put down, I feel I should actually have rewritten many parts of the story. First of all, I remembered later many details that were missing in my story.

Above all else, I have the impression that I put too much emphasis in telling about the modesty and uniformity of life in my parents' home. It may appear as if I wanted to say that life was friendless at our house. Actually, enjoyment was given much room in our life. As the four sisters got married at an early age, we were at that point more ready to absorb and accept social and other pleasures. What I realized only later was the extent to which this gave us freedom. The exemplary harmony of our parents' marriage influenced our marriages as well.

My mother was the ideal comrade for my father. She did not have to fight for equality. Father often referred to her as his "companion." We never heard a sharp word exchanged between our parents. What this balanced approach meant for the children, I realized only much later when I saw other couples where this was not always the case. Our development was also affected by our family's improving economic level. This allowed the children to enjoy an ascending living standard. We learned to appreciate this fully only in light of the events during the years since the beginning of the war [*World War I*].

If I am now able, through the loving effort of Susi [*Hedwig's daughter-in-law Susan Brodnitz, wife of Heinz*], to share these lines, which were originally only meant for Julius, with my children, it may be appropriate to add a time line to these notes. My parents are well remembered by my children. I am not sure, however, that they know that my father, Abraham Herzfeld was born on June 8, 1836, in Graetz and that he died on December 23, 1907, in Berlin. I am not sure whether my children know that my mother, Julia, born Badt, was born in Graefenhain in Schles, on November 25, 1848, and followed her husband on July 11, 1914 [*in Berlin*]. Of the ten children born to this couple, six survived and will, I hope, be with us for a long time to come. The following are my surviving siblings:

- Rosa, born on June 12, 1871, married [*Hugo Brodnitz*] on December 17, 1889.
- Helene [*Lenchen*], born on September 21, 1873, married [*Samuel Meyer*] on August 22, 1893.

- Salomon (known since high school as Ernst), born on February 14, 1875, married [*Klara Frankensein*] on December 25, 1904.
- Hugo, born on April 2, 1881, married [*Grete Leyens*] on April 18, 1920.
- Bianka, born on July 8, 1883, married [*Hermann Brodnitz*] on May 15, 1904.

Notes

Hedwig Herzfeld Brodnitz was born on June 22, 1878, in Graetz, Province of Posen, Germany, and died on October 29, 1938, in New York City. She was the wife of Julius (1866–1936) and mother of

- Friedrich (Fritz) Brodnitz (1899–1995)
- Otto Brodnitz (1902–1976)
- Heinz Brodnitz (1905–1984)

The original manuscript of Hedwig's memoir

Epilogue
Julius and Hedwig Brodnitz
by Michael Brodnitz

WHEN MY GRANDMOTHER HEDWIG finished the original version of her memoir, she added a handwritten dedication, dated October 30, 1923. In it she noted that her story was written for her husband, Julius, on the occasion of the twenty-fifth anniversary of their marriage. She stated that she had written her story during a very hard time, as the years between the end of World War I (November 1918) and the Great Depression of 1929 were, indeed, very difficult in much of the world. This was especially the case in Germany, where runaway inflation had wiped out most of the savings and financial assets of middle class citizens. Hedwig noted that she started recording her memories while she was recovering from an illness in the spring of 1921. Her story was dedicated to the memory of her parents, Abraham and Julie Herzfeld.

In the summer of 1931, Hedwig, with the help of her daughter-in-law Susi, prepared additional copies of her memoir for Hedwig's three sons, Fritz, Otto, and Heinz. Susi Behrend married Hedwig's youngest son, Heinz, in May 1931. In those days, before the advent of electronic copying devices, preparing additional copies required repeated retyping of the manuscript on a manual typewriter. Hedwig used this opportunity to add a postscript, which is included at the end of chapter 3.

Little could Julius or Hedwig have guessed that the coming years until their deaths (Julius in 1936 and Hedwig in 1938) would be the most dramatic and eventful period of their lives. We know a little about some of the events of those days because Grandpa Julius kept a diary, which his oldest son, Fritz, brought with him in late 1937 when he left Germany for the United States. Every evening, Julius noted his key activities and observations for that day in his diary. We don't know when Julius began this habit, but we found some pages of older diaries going back to the year 1917. We also located Julius' bound diaries for the years 1933 to 1936. The last book ended when Julius was fatally injured, hit by a car while crossing a street on his way to visit Hedwig, who was recovering from an operation.

In my parents' apartment in Tel Aviv, we located several dozen letters that Julius and Hedwig had mailed to their son Heinz and his wife, Susi, during the years after they immigrated to Palestine, he in late 1933 and she in early 1934, respectively. Most of these letters were handwritten weekly communications from Hedwig to her children. They were written on thin paper, which was commonly used in those days to save on airmail postage. Some of her letters were written using carbon paper so that she could mail separate copies to each of her three sons. This adds to the difficulty of reading and translating many of Hedwig's letters.

From Julius' diary, we know of two events that reshaped the lives of his two younger sons, Otto and Heinz, who lost their jobs in 1930. Otto was employed as an economist at a respectable bank in Berlin. In the late 1920s, he was let go by his employer at a time when the economy had taken a sharp downturn. After a futile search for a job in Germany, Otto immigrated to the United States and settled in New York City. His first years there were not always easy, but he managed to find employment until the U.S. economy improved at the end of the decade.

Heinz completed his academic training and was employed as an engineer at the large German operation of the I. G. Farben organization. When he took a vacation day to celebrate Yom Kippur, his employer realized that Heinz was a Jew and promptly fired him. Heinz was more fortunate than his brother, however, and located a position as chief engineer in a factory in the town of Neisse, where he stayed until the plant was nationalized by the Nazis in early 1933.

German federal elections took place on September 14, 1930, following a bitter campaign. Julius Brodnitz foresaw the dangers that a Nazi success would bring and campaigned vigorously, urging Germany's Jews to come out and vote for the opposition to Hitler's party. A speech, which Julius delivered on September 14, 1930, was recorded. In that speech, Julius warned that the small Jewish community in Germany must stand up against the impending dangers. He finished his speech saying "none of us believe that the problems that face us will be resolved on the fourteenth of September.... If we have the interest and help of all our friends in the country, if we succeed in expanding and strengthening our organization, if we mean something in the political life of Germany, then the hour will not be too far when all these difficulties will be finally conquered." Appendix A is the complete translation of that speech.

In the election of 1930, the NSDAP (Nazi Party) under the leadership of Adolf Hitler, won 107 seats in the Reichstag (the German Parliament). This made the Nazis into the second largest party in the new House, but it kept them from gaining control of the government.

On January 1, 1931, Julius looked back at the events of the past year and noted:

> In all of Germany and in almost the whole world, one looks at the coming year with concerns. The poor economic situation, especially during the last quarter of the past year, impacted also our financial situation. I had worked in my profession all through the year. The results were relatively favorable. Fritz, like most people, suffered setbacks in his medical practice during the last quarter of the year. Considering his age, he is seriously affected by it. Otto has a difficult situation in the USA. He has to be very happy that he

has a job, even if it is a rather limited position. Heinz has had a good year in Neisse, from both the professional and personal aspects. Fortunately, we found out that we were spared additional sickness so that we could all fulfill our duties. A bright spot was our agreement with Susi's family [*regarding the impending wedding of Heinz and Susi*]. May that be a good omen for the coming year.

The following year, on January 1, 1932, Julius noted:

> The concerns that we had at the beginning of the past year have not disappeared but rather have become even more pronounced. Are we getting closer to the end of the crises? Our closest circle and we were spared during the past year. Except for my passing illness, we have all stayed healthy. Susi and Heinz have been a great joy [*they were married in late May, 1931, in Berlin*]. Fritz managed reasonably well. Otto is able to support himself, even if only in a limited way. Rosa is suffering economically [*she was Hedwig's oldest sister and the widow of Hugo Brodnitz, Julius' older brother*]. May the coming year turn out better than we now fear!

During the days of the Weimar Republic, Germany commemorated Constitution Day by having citizens display the national tricolor flag from both public and private buildings. Julius and Hedwig followed that tradition. The Nazis, however, hated the Republic and all its institutions. They refused to fly the tricolored national flag and honored only their own red and black Nazi banners. In mid morning on Constitution Day, 1932, someone phoned the Brodnitz flat in Berlin and ordered Julius and Hedwig to remove the national flag, which they were flying from their balcony, and to fly the Nazi flag instead. The Brodnitz couple had moved into their flat only recently, and the phone number had not yet been listed in the public phone book, so this threatening phone call came to them as a surprise. When they refused to follow the Nazi's instructions, they received a letter in their mailbox that repeated this threat. Thereupon, Julius Brodnitz wrote to the chief of Section I of the Police Department in Berlin [*we know about this because Julius saved a handwritten copy of this letter along with a certified mail receipt dated August 20, 1932*]. Both letters are still in the family's possession.

We do not know whether Julius received any answer from the Berlin Police Department. We do know, however, that the Nazi Party operated a local office near the Brodnitz apartment on Prinzregenten Street in Berlin. It must have been a rather courageous act to disobey these people and to complain about their activities to the authorities.

On January 1, 1933, Julius noted:

> The past year did not turn out as badly as we had feared. We have stayed healthy and alive. Our children made it through the year in a reasonable fashion. Otto has enjoyed a substantial step forward in his career. There is a reasonable chance that he will be coming for a visit to Germany in the coming spring [*we know that Otto visited Germany in late March of 1933; during that visit, he helped Julius compose telegrams, which were sent to key Jewish leaders in the United States, requesting that they mellow their anti-German boycott*]. Our Rosa died as a result of the worries of these times. The difficulties of the times were noticeable in the results of my work during the last half of the year. The coming year stands before us full of question marks. May the circle of these questions get resolved in a more or less satisfactory fashion.

We possess three sources about the events of the months that followed and the role that Julius and Hedwig played in them. We have Julius' diary in which he wrote fairly detailed notes about the events of the day, so we know of his major activities during that horrible period. From the diary we see how difficult the year

1933 turned out to be for Julius as well as for the whole German-Jewish community. We read, for example that twice during the month of March, Julius was summoned to the office of Minister Goering, one of Hitler's top deputies who, in 1933, was put in charge of the German State of Brandenburg, which includes the city of Berlin.

The first meeting took place on March 3. It followed a search of the C.V.'s head office on the evening of March 1 by a group of Schutzstaffel (SS) men. The SS also arrested a number of C.V. leaders who happened to be in the office at that time. The stated reason for the search was that the Nazis had supposedly obtained information about weapons or explosives that were supposed to have been hidden in that facility. Of course, nothing like that was true, and nothing illegal was found the office. According to Julius, Goering was very friendly to the C.V. leaders when they reported to his office and stated that it was silly to think that the C.V. would be a hiding place for anti-Nazi weapons.

On March 25, Julius was again summoned to Goering's office. On this occasion, three other leaders of the Jews in Berlin were also present. According to Julius, this time Goering was a "changed man." He ordered the Jewish leaders to contact their counterparts in the United States and stop anti-German rallies that were scheduled to take place in New York and in other locations on the following weekend. We know from Julius' diary that he and his second son, Otto, who had just arrived in Berlin from New York on a business trip, spent the rest of that evening composing and sending telegrams to the Jewish leaders in the United States regarding the anti-German gatherings.

From the diary we also know that Julius had several meetings with leaders of the non-Nazi parties, who were part of Hitler's governing coalition in the Reichstag. As we know from history, those groups gradually lost whatever limited influence they thought they had on the Nazis, and they did little to help the German-Jewish community.

According to the entries in the diary, Julius traveled to at least ten major German cities during 1933: Köln in the west of Germany to Stettin in the east and then to Neisse in the southeast of Germany. In all of these places, he met with the local leaders of the C.V. to learn about anti-Jewish activities in their area. Usually these visits also included large public meetings in which the local Jewish population was updated on pending national events.

During the first half of 1933, Julius noted in his diary that more than forty meetings and discussions had related to his role as president of the C.V. He also met with other leaders of the German-Jewish community in an effort to form an overarching organization that would represent all the major Jewish groups in Germany. This organization was eventually formed. It was initially called *Die Reichsvertretung* (the National Representation of the German Jews). It was presided over by Julius' colleague Rabbi Leo Baeck [*the Baeck Institutes in Jerusalem, London, and New York were named after Rabbi Baeck*].

In addition to these duties, Julius attempted to continue his professional life as a lawyer and notary. On July 1, 1933, the Nazis published a legal notice that "released" Dr. Brodnitz from his function as a public notary. This led, "with a heavy heart," to the dissolution of Julius' law partnership, which had lasted for more than twenty-six years. To save on expenses, Julius relocated his office to his own apartment.

As 1933 progressed, the wording of the entries to the diary gradually became more and more guarded. Whereas formerly Julius would identify his contacts in the diary by their names and affiliations, later entries in the diary just said, "meeting with our friends."

In addition to his Jewish and C.V. responsibilities, Julius and Hedwig were also the focal point of extensive family activities. On more than sixty days during 1933, Julius' recorded in the diary that relatives came to the elder Brodnitz's for lunch or dinner. All in all, well over one hundred members of Julius and Hedwig's extended family joined them for one or more meals.

Younger members of the expanded family often visited Julius to seek his advice. We don't know what Julius told these visitors, but it is a fact that all but one of these younger relatives departed from Germany early enough to find a safe haven beyond the reach of the Nazis. Two younger lawyers, Peter Brodnitz [*son of Dr. Siegfried Brodnitz*] and Heini Kronstein [*husband of their niece Kate Brodnitz*], looked for advice as to what they should do when the Nazis barred young non-Aryans from practicing law in Germany. Both left the country within a short time.

Julius must have felt that there was no future for young Jews in Hitler's Germany. On January 1, 1934, The diary reads:

> A year full of worries and a forecast full of concerns! Our dear Hugo Herzfeld [*Hedwig's brother*] was taken from us during this year, and Ludwig Tietz [*Fritz's friend and one of the leaders of the Jewish youth group of the C.V.*] also departed. Our children, with the exception of Otto, had lost their places of work. My law partnership was dissolved. We do not want to give up hope.

What Julius did not mention in his year-end review was that by November 20, 1933, his youngest son, Heinz, left Germany for Palestine. Heinz had lost his job in Niesse in early 1933. His wife, Susi, had to stop her studies at the University of Dresden when her thesis advisor, who was Jewish, lost his job and left Germany for a position at Dartmouth College in the United States. Susi followed Heinz to Palestine in March of 1934.

About one month later, on April 25, 1934, Julius and Hedwig traveled to Amsterdam. While there they met with several people, including their son Fritz. The entry for April 28 reads cryptically, "Morning, dictating to Hedwig." In the evening of the following day, April 29, they returned to Berlin.

Many years later, after Fritz's death, we located a copy in Fritz's desk in New York of what Julius had dictated to Hedwig on April

28, 1934, while away from Germany in Amsterdam. These ten pages of handwritten notes, written in Hedwig Brodnitz's handwriting, were not signed. At the bottom of the last page is an inscription: "Amsterdam 28.4.34." In these pages, Julius summarizes his recollections of the key events of the first year of Hitler's rule in Germany. Appendix B is a complete translation of these notes.

On January 1, 1935, Julius wrote in his diary:

> It could have turned out even worse. The future is full of worries. However, we do not despair. We have met with Otto again. He is still in a position, which, considering the situation, is rather fortunate. Fritz has satisfying Jewish work, although he has not found a way to go back to his former position [*as a medical doctor*]. Susi and Heinz are leading a satisfactory life in Palestine, although it is not easy for them. We have stayed in relatively good health, and we are carrying our fate together and with dignity. Professionally I had the good luck to adjust to the circumstances. We were able to feed ourselves, and I also had some satisfaction from it. I was also able to fulfill my Jewish obligations.

The entry for the following year, written on January 1, 1936, was less optimistic. Julius noted:

> The year begins in gloomy fashion. The last half of this year [*1935*] has seen our situation become even gloomier. This year brought us our grandson [*Michael*]. We have remained healthy and have passed the difficult challenges. I passed my operation successfully. Our children who live overseas [*Otto and Heinz*] have brought us happiness. A dark cloud sits as far as the coming year is concerned. Hedwig has assumed additional responsibilities in running the household. She did so with courage and determination [*apparently, they could no longer afford to employ household help*]. The future path for

Fritz is unknown. All of us want to keep marching on our assigned paths with dignity.

On March 6, 1936, Julius and Hedwig sailed from Trieste, Italy, to Palestine. When their ship arrived in the port of Haifa on March 13, their youngest son, Heinz, met them. Although their stay in Palestine included the Passover week, there is no reference in the diary to a celebration of the holiday. The diary mentions a lengthy list of the Jewish leaders in Palestine with whom Julius met during his visit. As the president of the C.V., Julius never joined any Zionist group. Nonetheless, during his visit to Palestine, several of the major Zionist leaders in that country took the time to meet and dine with him.

From a letter which Julius and Hedwig posted from Palestine during their visit, we also know that in spite of the so-called Arab Rebellion of 1936 to 1939 (which began while they visited Palestine), both were very impressed by what they saw during their visit and intended to return to that country as soon as they could.

In a letter mailed to Fritz at the midpoint of their stay [*dated April 1, 1936*], Julius notes, "One still has to digest the great and wide-ranging impressions in order not to rush to a judgment. In any case, what one experiences here is certainly something big." Grandma Hedwig added, "The child is really a joy, and I am sure this magnet, more than anything else, will pull us back to this place [*in fact, only Hedwig returned to Palestine*].

Julius' last two letters to his son Heinz were written shortly after his return from Palestine. In both of these letters, Julius writes almost like a convinced Zionist. In Julius' letter of May 12, 1936, he noted, "As a result of my visit, I have concluded that the unique experiment that is Eretz Israel, in spite of its many problems, must not fail or else it would cause irreparable damage to Judaism in the whole world.... As long as this pioneering spirit prevails among the immigrants [*to Palestine*], then the hope is justified...that this work would not be in vain." In Julius' last letter, dated June 9, 1936, he wrote that he had managed to get the approval of the Reichsvertretung [*the leadership group of the Jews in Germany, of which he was a member*] to contribute 200.000 Reichmarks to the Keren Hayesod [*the Jewish Agency for Palestine*] for projects in Palestine.

On June 4, Hedwig underwent an operation in a clinic in Berlin. All went well, but she required hospitalization for the next two weeks. In spite of his heavy workload and his own questionable health, Julius came to visit her daily. On June 16, 1936, while crossing a street near Hedwig's hospital, Julius was struck by a car and suffered a concussion. He was taken to the same hospital where Hedwig was already recovering. His condition deteriorated, and on June 17, 1936, he died from his injuries.

Fritz collected and saved copies of numerous obituaries that were published in Jewish and general-circulation newspapers. Included in the collection are an obituary in the New York Times of June 18, 1936, and many Jewish publications from around Germany and from several European papers.

Hedwig outlived Julius by about two years. During that time, she was clearly restless and upset by the events in the world around her.

From a letter that Hedwig mailed on August 15, 1936, we know that shortly after Julius' death, she met my parents, Heinz and Susi, in the Dolomites in Northern Italy. She had written to her son Fritz that she was expecting Heinz to arrive there within the week and suggested that Fritz might want to join them, which he did. In Tel Aviv and in Fritz's apartment in New York, we found photos that were taken by Fritz during that visit to the Dolomites.

Shortly after that reunion, Hedwig traveled to New York to visit with her third son, Otto. From immigration records, we believe that she arrived at the Port of New York on October 6, 1936.

Upon returning to Berlin, Hedwig applied for an Immigration Visa to Palestine. The British Government controlled Palestine at that time under a Mandate from the League of Nations.

They allowed only a very limited number of Jews to enter the country each year. An exception was, however made for people who qualified for a visa under the so-called Capitalist Quota. To qualify for such a visa, one had to prove that one possessed at least 1,000 British Pounds, which was at that time a princely amount of money.

The Nazi Government severely restricted what Jews could take with them when they left Germany. They did, however, make an agreement with the Zionist Organization in Palestine under which German Jews deposited German Marks of a value equal to 1,000 Pounds with an organization by the name of Haavara Ltd. Haavara used these Marks to purchased German manufactured goods that were needed in Palestine. These items were then sold in Palestine, and payment was made to the immigrant in an equal amount of Palestine Pounds. We located several documents that pertain to Hedwig's communications with Haavara regarding these transactions.

Hedwig sent some of her furniture from Berlin to Tel Aviv, where she rented a modest apartment near the apartment in which Heinz and his family were living. There she tried to make a new life for herself. We know very little about Hedwig's stay in Palestine. The period of 1936 to 1939 is known as the Arab Rebellion. The Arab citizens of Palestine were constantly attacking the country's Jewish residents as well as the British police and army. The country's economy was under stress following the worldwide economic collapse of the financial markets in 1929, and the local Arabs attempted to get the British authorities to stop the Jewish immigration, which was on the rise in response to European anti-Semitism.

Hedwig's youngest son, Heinz, was earning a meager living and supporting his young family by designing electric systems for architects who were constructing major projects, such as the Government Hospital in Haifa. To augment his income, Heinz also repaired refrigerators in a corner of his small apartment.

In 1938, Heinz was offered a professional position at the Palestine Economic Corporation. The position was respectable and removed the need for a side job from his life. However, accepting this position required the relocation of the family to Jerusalem.

In the meantime, in 1937, Hedwig's oldest son, Fritz, escaped from Germany. After a period of several months during which he decompressed by working for the Jewish Joint Relief organization in Paris, Fritz immigrated to the United States. We don't know what triggered Hedwig's next move; from Hedwig's German Passport, we know that in June of 1938, Hedwig sailed from the port of Haifa to Marseille, France. She then transited through Belgium and the Netherlands to the UK. She next sailed on to New York, where she landed on August 23, 1938. At the time of her arrival, she was granted a Visitor's Visa, valid for a stay in the United States until October 11, 1938.

When Hedwig arrived, the United States was in the midst of the Great Depression. Neither she nor her sons Fritz and Otto were well off financially. Fritz was studying English and getting ready for a test in American medical terminology, which he had to pass before he could be certified as a medical doctor in the United States.

His younger brother, Otto, had a position as the personal assistant to Mr. Henry Goldman. This was considered a good position in those days but one with only limited chances to advance [*a side note: For Fritz's application for a U.S. visa in 1937, Mr. Goldman provided him with a letter addressed to the U.S. Immigration Department in which Mr. Goldman listed his own occupation as "retired banker" and stated that he possessed "materially in excess of $1,000,000"*].

Hedwig's stay in New York coincided with the meeting of the British prime minister (Neville Chamberlain), the French prime minister (Édouard Daladier), Benito Mussolini, and Adolf Hitler at Berchtesgaden, during which Britain and France agreed to partition Czechoslovakia and let Germany annex the Sudetenland.

Chamberlain agreed to Hitler's demands and returned to London claiming that he had achieved "peace for our time." Hitler, of course, broke the agreement within a few months and occupied the rest of Czechoslovakia in March 1939, something Hedwig did not live to see.

In one of Hedwig's last letters, dated October 5, 1938, she described the recent events, as she followed them from New York:

> Now that the so-called "peace" broke out again, I find the nerves to sit and write. The atmosphere, which was already dramatic and exciting enough, became ever more charged with electricity by the never-ending radio reports, which broadcast directly from Europe [*intercontinental broadcasting was a recent innovation that had begun at the time of crisis of 1938*]. Whenever one failed to listen to the radio for one or two hours, one felt as if one had committed a serious mistake. The print size of the headlines of the newspapers is becoming slowly a bit smaller and "less alarming." Those of us who are "Former European" can imagine what is behind the so-called "peace" declarations, and we know that now a new chapter of tears and misfortune is about to begin. The Czech will be treated as the Jews, in as much as they are now forced to depend on hope and promises that were made to them. An argument that is frequently used here, in consolation, states that even Napoleon eventually had a bad fall. I find that rather unhelpful. Hopefully, you'll live long enough to see the day when Europe discovers again its friendly face. I will certainly not.

Hedwig was, of course, proven right in her observations. She died in New York City on October 29, 1938, without seeing Hitler's fall from power. Per her wishes, she was buried next to her late husband, Julius, in the Jewish Cemetery in Potsdam, near Berlin, where the headstone marks their joint resting place.

Epilogue 211

Last family portrait in Berlin, 1933

Julius Brodnitz, meeting of the Advisory Council of the Reichsvertretung on October 14, 1934

Julius Brodnitz during his last public appearance. He was one of the speakers at a meeting that was organized by the Jewish Agency to protest against the Arab terror in Palestine, which took place on April 29, 1936. (Julius had recently returned from visiting Heinz, Susi, and Michael Brodnitz in Palestine.)

Appendix A
Julius Brodnitz's Speech, August 1930

The following speech was delivered in August 1930 by Julius Brodnitz (Chairman of the Centralverein deutscher Staatsbuerger juedischen Glaubens, aka the C.V.) during the election campaign of September 14, 1930. This election was the first of three federal elections to the Reichstag that were held in Germany between 1930 and 1932. In none of these elections did a single party win enough votes to control a majority in the House. In the election of September 14, 1930, the SPD (Socialist) won 143 seats, down from 153 in the previous Reichstag. The NSDAP (Nazi) won 107 seats (up from only 12 in the old House), and the KPD (Communist) also gained 23 seats (from 54 to 77 seats). None of these parties could put together the block of 289 seats needed for a majority in the Reichstag. As a result of this gridlock, President Hindenburg asked leaders of smaller center parties to form the government. These governments could not get the support of a majority in the Reichstag nor pass any budgets or laws.

In the last free election of the Weimer Republic, which was held on November 6, 1932, again, none of the parties got a majority. Finally, on January 30, 1933, President Hindenburg asked Hitler to form a government. The Nazis, with the support of several smaller center-right parties, were able to get a majority in the Reichstag. A short time later, the Nazis called for new elections, which were neither open nor free, and they never again had to face any free elections until they were defeated by the Allies in May of 1945.

Who among you, my Jewish friends, does not recognize the demands of these hours, in the current period of most serious threats, at a time that, in its seriousness and its tragic aspects, has not existed for many many tens of years?

Only by the unconditional activation of all our resources can we succeed in being protected from the danger that is facing us!

A great many of you are blind to these dangers or believe that we, a small minority, cannot accomplish anything against the great majority.

Completely wrong! Only he who gives up on himself is lost. The whole history of our Jewish community is a single outstanding proof that there is a force greater than all external dangers—the will to live! This we must uphold! This we must preserve if we want to provide a bright future for our children.

If we have been suffering severely, both economically and spiritually, then it must be attributed to a large extent to the National Socialists, who have created an atmosphere of agitation and hate against us. Against them in the first place we direct our opposition.

If we all, those who have a sunny or a moody disposition, battle together for the existence of Jewish rights and Jewish honor, and for the maintenance and strengthening of our economic position, we have no reason to despair.

Therefore, these are our actions today. Do not believe that we cannot achieve anything. We know what is needed to agitate in an election campaign and we'll use all of these means. A wide range of preparatory work has already been done. Your help and efforts will determine the extent to which our electoral means will have an effect! If we grow and rise to face the existing threats and dangers, we can be assured that the positively disposed part of the German people will align with our side.

None of us believe that the problems that face us will be resolved on the fourteenth of September. The fourteenth of September is only a step on the way for the difficult internal strife that faces our Fatherland. These too shall find us at our assigned posts. If we have the interest and help of all our friends in the country, if we succeed in expanding and strengthening our organization, if we mean something in the political life of Germany, then the hour will not be too far when all the difficulties are finally conquered.

Appendix B
Notes from Julius Brodnitz, 1934

Following is a translation of notes that were dictated by Julius Brodnitz to his wife, Hedwig, in Amsterdam on April 28, 1934. It contains the only known presentation of Julius' recollection of the events that followed Hitler's first year as leader of Germany.

Uncertainty in January about the negotiations between Papen-Hitler. 24.1.33 [*dates in notes follow Julius' European conventions, here January 24, 1933; Papen-Hitler refers to negotiations between Franz von Papen and Adolf Hitler*].

General meeting of the *Hilfsverein* [*Help Organization*] at Kaiserhof. This was also the headquarters of Hitler. The rooms that were set aside for the use of the Hilfsverein are closed off by members of the watch and guard groups.

January 29. The leadership of the C.V. assumes that the negotiations are failing because of the excessive demands of Hitler.

January 30. Werner [*possibly Callman*] reports from Munich that, based on conversations with a Bavarian delegate, the possibility of Hitler's appointment as Reichskanzler [*Prime Minister*] is not under consideration. During the conversation, the report reaches us that the appointment had occurred. Reichmann is considered very endangered [*Reichmann was one of the senior members of the permanent staff of the C.V.*]. He has located himself outside of Berlin. At that time, Munich was still considered as a safe place.

February 14 and 15. On the fourteenth and fifteenth of February, I held big gatherings in Krefeld and in Aachen. In the last minute, Kr [*possibly leaders in Krefeld*] got rather frightened, but decided to hold the meeting in any case. At that time it was the general opinion that Hitler was building his government on the basis of the large industrial concerns and leading the workers by the nose.

February 22. Presidential discussions with Oscar Wassermann. It is claimed that H. [*perhaps Hindenburg, president of Germany*] said with regard to Goebbels: "A drummer does not get to be a general."

March 1. As the news of the death of Hugo Herzfeld [*the eldest brother of Hedwig Brodnitz*] reached our office, we got the news of a house search in the C.V. and the arrests. Ongoing negotiations.

March 2. Request by phone from Diehl to come to a meeting with Göering. In reply to questions by D., it appears that he wanted to speak to me.

March 3. An hour-long discussion with Göering, while Hugo was getting buried. G. plays only the sweetest notes of peace. The suspicion that C.V. is taking part in the Communist actions was a "paradox."

Sunday, March 5. While the election results are announced on the radio, it is announced that the C.V. was outlawed in Thuringen [*a German state*], because of "activities of high treason."

On March 1, with my concurrence, Hollaender disappeared. The condition of his health made it impossible to stand up to the dangers and excitements. Unfortunately, Hollaender carelessly went away while keeping the purpose of his trip a secret.

March 6. Hollaender and his wife appear desperately in my place. There was no choice but to suggest that they go openly with the declaration of the purpose of his going to a health facility.

March 13. Working party meeting after consultation with Baruch, Hollaender, Hirschberg, and Tietz.... Hollaender must leave because we cannot justify his staying, because of his health condition.

Repeated conversations with Captain Knaepper. The Dtsh-Nationalen [*German National Party*] want to believe that they are maintaining the upper hand and, if need be, they could push Hitler against the wall.

March 23. Arrival of Otto [*Brodnitz*].

March 25. Göering calls a meeting with the leaders of the various Jewish organizations in his office. We are received in a dictator-like fashion, with him surrounded by a large number of civil servants. From the beginning, it is clear that he receives us with the clear intention to only issue to us orders that the boycott [*of Germany and of imported German goods, organized by the Jewish leaders in the United States and in the United Kingdom*] outside the country must be terminated. The discussion took a different turn from the original intention. For about one hour, the discussion was about steps that could take place, if needed. On the prior day, without any steps on their part, at our own initiative, a report appeared in the *C.V.-Zeitung* about the first meeting with G. [*Göering*]. During the entire day, until late at night, with the help of Otto, a cable to the United States was put together [*they asked the Jewish leaders in the United States and United Kingdom to tone down their confrontation with Germany*].

March 26. Decision is made to send Tietz to London.

March 27. Late in the evening called to the Jewish Community building to advise regarding the threatened boycott of Jewish enterprises in Germany [*the Nazi government of Germany asked their citizens to boycott all Jewish enterprises in Germany on April 1, 1933*]. It was agreed not to issue any further statements on this matter. Emphatic report on the radio tells about the positive outcome of the meeting in New York [*this was the mass meeting in New York, protesting against the Nazi boycott*].

March 29. Early in the morning, a report on the radio that the boycott of Jewish enterprises scheduled for April 1 was announced.

April 1. Boycott of Jewish enterprises.

April 6 and the following days. Ongoing discussions regarding the Lawyer's Law. Anticipated restriction of the number of Jewish lawyers in Berlin to thirty.

April 13 [18??]. Lawyer's Law is announced. Daily presidential conversations [*possibly at the C.V.*].

April 28. Conference with State Secretary von Buelow. He is very thankful for the developments outside the country. He also requests continuation of activity outside the country.

Wiener disappears several times. Supposedly because of discussions on the border with Holland. Also on April 1 after he blubbered bitterly, as I was told only after the fact, in front of Fritz [*Brodnitz?*] and Tietz.

May 9. As it turned out later, without success, the restriction on representation becomes effective.

May 23. Meeting in Reich Justice Ministry with Ministry Consultant Jonas regarding the setting aside of injustice versus the old notaries. No chance of mitigation. Weekly consultations with Baeck, Melchior, Tietz, Loewenstein, Blumenfeld.

June 6. Conference with Hollaender because of his contractual relationship. He himself agreed that he could not work at this time, wants to go on trips.

June 10. Reception at our place honoring Willstaedter and Frank because of the formation of the Reichsvertretung [*the umbrella organization for the German-Jewish community, of which Julius Brodnitz was a member*].

June 13. New conversations with Hollaender about the old topic [*this had to do with the question of Mr. H's retirement from his position at the C.V. because he could not continue to function under the pressure put on the organization by the Nazis*]. On June 2, in connection with the Reichskollegum, serious discussions between Tietz, Wiener, and myself regarding various diplomatic activities also aimed at me personally [*the Jewish leadership in Germany was under constant pressure by the Nazi government*]. Wiener gave notice shortly after that, but he let it rest for the time being. Repeated conversations with foreign friends. On June 23 and 29, noteworthy information about the dissolution of the C.V. together with many or all Jewish organizations.

June 29. According to Tietz's information from the Belgian Consulate, the C.V. will be dissolved. On the previous evening, Wiener came to me. He was crying bitterly and said that he was feeling as he did during the war [*World War I*], during the retreat from Palestine. He was no longer bodily or emotionally able to work in Germany. Time off, based on health reasons was granted. Wiener stated that it was impossible for him to take part in the important meeting that was scheduled for June 29. With time, political peace ensued, so that I decided to go on vacation. Officially (I went) to Neisse, which I could reach in an hour from Moessnig in Czechoslovakia.

All along, the decisive developments with Weiner and especially before June 28, when his letter giving notice was completely ignored, I was trying to prevent this while Hollaender, who was constantly on trips, wanted to pick up his workload. Herzfeld succeeded in getting Hollaender to come to him in Essen before returning. They agreed that Hollaender would devote all his time only to caring for his health.

July 31. Visit in Neisse by Weiner. He declared that in spite of the current quieter conditions, he cannot again pick up his role in the legal case of Marx in Frankfurt. I convinced Wiener to go to Dr. Reinhold in Graefenburg for consultation. R. reported that in peaceful conditions, outside Germany, Wiener could recover, so it would be good to convince Wiener to move to calmer circumstances.

Wiener goes on further vacation. After coming back, he negotiates with Wallach, Borchardt regarding indemnification. Thereafter, Wiener goes out of the country and, except for one short visit, does not return anymore.

I have several files regarding the developments in Hollaender's retirement case.

November 4. The death of Ludwig Tietz.

November 5. Sad revelations from Walter Tietz.

November 8. Discussions with Wiener-Berlak. Wiener returns for a few days in order to work out some financial issues. Issues resolved in a friendly manner.

December 16. On the day before the meeting of the Advisory Council, Krombach and Gallinger came to me, pushed by Hollaender. At the Advisory Council meeting, Wallach put a letter in front of me in which he stated that I caused his loss of influence because of my own financial considerations. At the Advisory Board meeting, I was appalled by the mental condition and attitude of Hollaender who turns to the whole world and wants a damage claim to be heard under the supervision of Stahl [*Hollaender tried to get Mr. Stahl, who was not a member of the C.V., involved in his claim for a bigger retirement pension from the C.V.*]. The Advisory placed the case in the hands of Krombach, Ernst Herzfeld, Berlak, and Gallinger, who accepted the known agreement with Hollaender, which is to be found in my files. Hollaender is to participate in the Working Party and Advisory Board. Except for rare encounters in the meeting room, all our communications have been only in the form of letters. After that, Hollaender resigned from the *Liberal Jewish Newspaper*. At my reproach, he used a harmless process to announce his retirement. He demanded that this be published in a more vigorous form. The publication was made mellower through my interference.

In the months since then, the activities in big meetings have greatly diminished. I spoke at a large gathering in Berlin on November 13 [*1933*] and have also spoken at numerous communities since that date.

First meeting with Göering took place without the presence of a third party. The second meeting we were made to stand. I requested to sit, whereupon chairs were provided for all. Naumann was surprised that Blumenfeld [*the Zionist leader*] was also invited. He wanted at first to leave but stayed nonetheless. Before the meeting, a very unpleasant discussion with Jacob Goldschmidt, who declared, against our vigorous disagreement (by Weiner and me) that only Naumann could speak for us.

They claimed that the C.V. was discredited. During the search of the home of Wassermann, all interventions were turned down. Jacob Goldschmidt wanted to be involved. Unchanged and courageous work by Reichmann and Hirschberg. Only after the fact, I learned from R. A. Luss-Dortmund that Weiner, with the approval of Luss, in an excited state, negotiated a Jewish concord, which did not get any further in the conversation than to state that one could no longer stay in Germany. Weiner tried to declare that his German point of view no longer had a foundation in the C.V. Before he left the country, there was never a word spoken on this topic.

Amsterdam April 28, 1934

www.ingramcontent.com/pod-product-compliance
Lightning Source LLC
Chambersburg PA
CBHW071729080526
44588CB00013B/1953